HER TIME

ANN JARMY

A THIRD FLEET CONVICT

LISA APFEL

ISBN: 978-1-7636376-0-3

Self-published by Lisa Apfel

Cover design by Lisa Apfel

For Andy

CONTENTS

ILLUSTRATIONS

Warning to Aboriginal and Torres Strait Islander peoples.

* * Members of Aboriginal and Torres Strait Islander communities are respectfully advised that this book contains references to historical violence and includes images of people who have passed away.*

Author's Apology:

To the descendants of the Dharug people who were killed, attacked and forced from their land by my ancestors either directly or indirectly I am sorry. I hope this book goes some way to truth telling. I have done my best to sift through the one-sided colonial accounts and combine them with Dharug information that is available about the events at Dyarubbin mentioned in this book.

Author's Notes

My notations are in square brackets.

Measurements

This book preserves contemporary units of measurement.

There were twelve pence to a shilling and twenty shillings to a pound.

One acre is equivalent to 0.405 hectares.

A mile is about 1.61 kilometres, and a foot is 30.5 centimetres.

In weight a pound is about 0.45 kilograms.

One bushel of wheat was equivalent to about 31 kilograms.

One imperial gallon equals 4.55 litres.

Symbols

Pre-decimal currency was written in the form:

£   Pound

s or /–   shillings

d   pence

INTRODUCTION

Curiosity, as usual, drove me. It was 1986 when I walked into the Family History Room of our brand-new library. The shelves of books were dust free and the microfilm readers shiny and new. It was intriguing. I scanned the titles, finding a few references here and there to familiar names my Nan had spoken about. Nothing earth shattering so I walked out.

I was sixteen with all the priorities in life that a sixteen-year-old has. Life moved on and all thoughts of the family history were gone. There was no internet in our lives. We had a couple of computers at school in the new computer room, which were available to the kids who wanted to learn about them. That definitely wasn't me. Playing with computers was considered social suicide and a sure way to be labelled a geek.

University came and computers advanced. I was dabbling with them. Exploring basic spreadsheets and word processors. Even being introduced to the concept of plugging a computer into my home landline so it could dial in and talk, to the computer at university. Mind blowing stuff.

University finished and work began, computers advanced and in 1996 we were on the World Wide Web with Netscape browser. Compared to struggling with code it was simple to use and literally bought the connected world to you. There were limited sites, but it was the start.

My family grew and parenting took centre stage. The internet advanced. Then one day in 1999, there I was at work, when I discovered the most amazing website that had come online, www.familysearch.org. The rest, as they say, is history.

A few searches and soon I was uncovering the names of my ancestors. The dig, the pursuit, the detective work, whatever you call it, was underway. Those few names that had lain dormant in my mind were suddenly the threads to opening this long-forgotten world. At first only basic information could be found, but it was enough to put me on the path that has since become my life's work.

I set myself a goal to find all my ancestors who came to Australia. I thought that would be easy. How wrong I was. It is a goal that still eludes me thanks to a couple of early arrivals who seem to have evaded the record keepers. What else would you expect from convicts!

I, like most Aussies, had this weird idea that having a convict in the family tree was a badge of honour. We have been brought up to think they were all hard done by, being sent out against their will for stealing a piece of bread. I soon realised that we were so wrong.

Like an archaeologist who finds some bones and then has to work out what this dinosaur looked like, I too have uncovered many, many bones. The result of which, I now have a good picture of who many of my ancestors were. They were the proverbial good, bad and ugly.

The women in particular touch my heart as their stories are invariably hidden behind their men. They were often viewed with disdain and thought of as inferior.

They had few avenues of recourse and often had to make the most of horrendous situations.

Within the following pages, you will encounter the reconstructed life story of Ann Jarmy, my five times great grandmother, who arrived in Australia as a convict. Because she is the earliest of my known ancestors to arrive, I wanted to tell her story first as a natural starting point. Her life is entwined in our colonial history and tells of hardships beyond measure.

She may not fit the traditional mould for a biographical subject, being relegated to the shadows of history as just another convict woman but it is precisely because of her obscurity that her story needs to be told. We have the biographies of the rich, the famous, the elite and the notorious, but we don't have many stories of the people. Who were these women, these wives, these mothers of our colonial born ancestors?

Tracing Ann's life has thrown up challenges. She was living at the earliest time in the colony when record keeping was often rudimentary. She was living in the remotest part of the colony where people could just disappear. Literacy levels were low, so that when records were taken, they were often filled with inaccuracies. This was evidenced by the various spellings of Ann's surname. I can picture her pronouncing it with a Norfolk accent and the record keeper writing what he heard. Her name is variously recorded as Jermy, Germain, Jermain, Germay, Germaine, German and peculiarly Jermoupu[1]. I have chosen to use the spelling as recorded on her baptism, Jarmy.

Discovering my lineage back to Ann came about after unravelling her daughter Sophia's link. Sophia was using the surname Bishop at her marriage and there were no matching birth records for a Sophia Bishop born in the colony that matched. The only record prior to the marriage that had her listed was the 1822 General Muster for New South Wales. She was fourteen and listed as a sister to Mrs. Bruce at Sydney and a servant to W. Bruce. Mrs. Bruce proved to be Maria Howell and her parents were Ann Germain and Samuel Howell. Great! So how did Sophia get the surname Bishop?

Two possibilities emerged. One was a forty-three-year-old, ex-marine of the First Fleet, named Elias Bishop. He was married and he and his wife had no children. He lived in the Richmond area where Ann was also living at the time Sophia was born.

The other was Bishop Thompson. Ann had known Bishop for a number of years, and she was known to be in a relationship with him three years prior when their son, Charles, was born. Having a clear link to him makes him the most likely.

The problem comes when explaining Sophia's use of the surname Bishop at the age of fourteen. Every other child of Ann's used their birth fathers' surnames. Why would Sophia change it? Perhaps the stain of having convict parents was too much.

In any event Ann is definitely my ancestor even if Sophia's father remains a mystery.

---

[1] Marsden, Samuel. 1806. 'Samuel Marsden Essays Concerning New South Wales, 1807-18--, with List of Females in the Colony, 1806?' State Library of NSW. https://collection.sl.nsw.gov.au/record/9O4olAAn.

The following is my representation of Ann's life based on many sources and facts. I have done my best to honour her memory and hope she can now come to life for you too.

CHAPTER 1
BORN INTO REBELLION

High on a hill in Norwich city's centre sat the towering Medieval Norwich Castle. Home to the Norfolk County gaol cells. Its glaring, white limestone walls had been a constant sight to the people of Norwich since 1120. In 1769, the year that Ann Jarmy was born, Norwich was the main city in county Norfolk, and it surpassed all other English cities in population except London. It boasted a newspaper, a bank, five hospitals, thirty-five churches, bowling greens and the assembly house where concerts, dances, and social gatherings were held.

Figure 1: View of Norwich with the Castle and on the Hill [2]

Although Norwich Castle was the geographic centre of the city, its beating heart was the medieval Norwich Market, that was said to be "one of the finest in England,"[3] being held every Wednesday and Saturday. With meat on open display, hawkers bellowing their deals, and a multitude of traders and entertainers vying for attention, it was a sensory assault. The vibrant energy was juxtaposed against the

[2] Cotman, Miles Edmund. n.d. *View of Norwich - YCBA Collections Search*. Yale Center for British Art, Paul Mellon Collection. Accessed 24 February 2024. https://collections.britishart.yale.edu/catalog/tms:8280.
[3] *The History and Antiquities of the County of Norfolk*. 1781. Norwich : Printed by J. Crouse for M. Booth. 222. http://archive.org/details/b28745401_0010.

neighbouring Guildhall, which housed the city's gaol cells. It's flint walls, the colour of a dark bruise, permeating the sorrow from within.

Surrounding the city were its flint walls, built to protect the people within. Along the walls were the gates that allowed passage in and out of the city. The gates were locked every night at 10pm.

Figure 2: Norwich. The central castle on its manmade mound and the city protected by the Wensum River and the wall and gates. "Courtesy of Aviva Group Archive"[4]

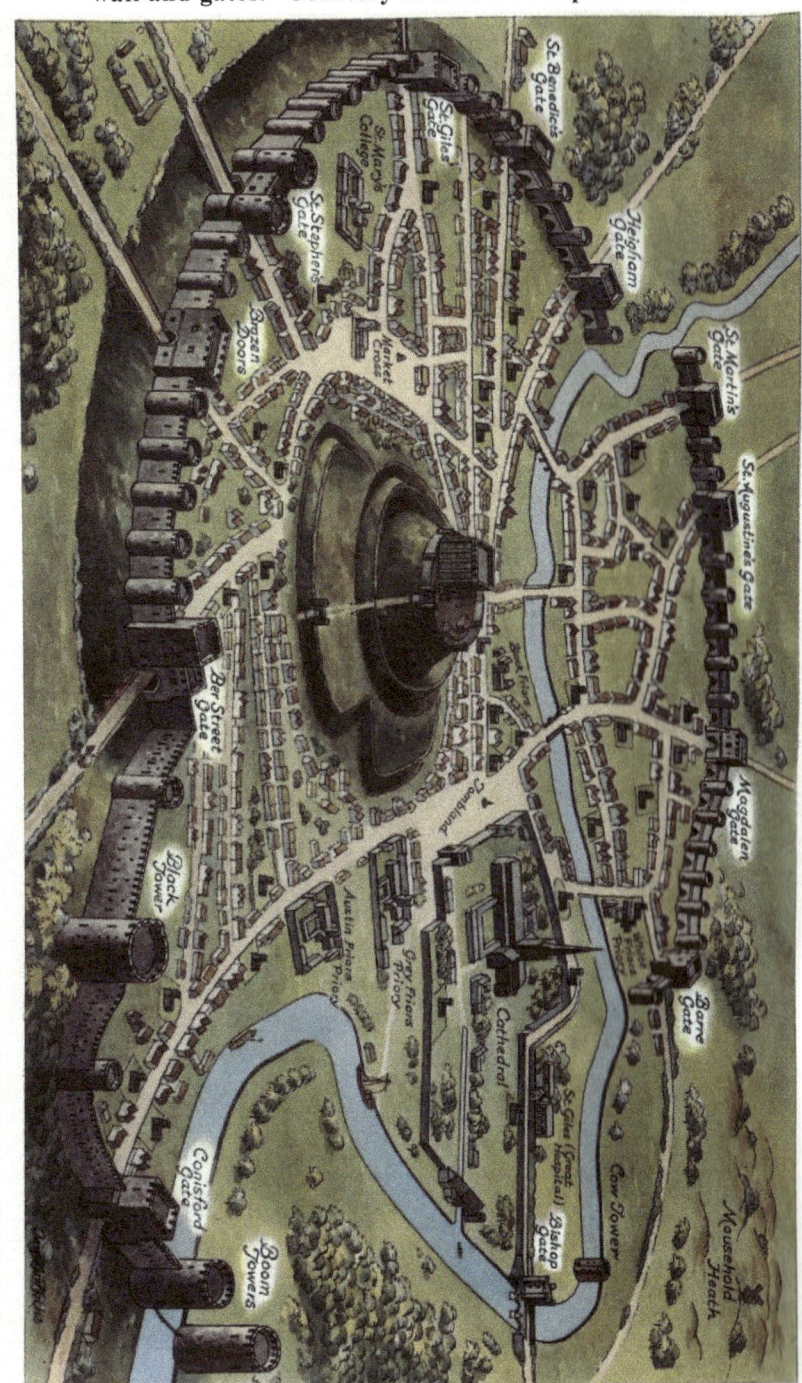

King George III and the white wig wearing wealthy aristocrats made all the political decisions. The commoners had no political voice. The king even chose the prime minister. The criminal law imposed harsh penalties, with thefts over forty shillings punishable by death. "The Slave Trade…[was] regarded as a legitimate commercial enterprise, and slavery itself as a respectable institution."[5] The tensions between Protestants and Catholics persisted, public education and public health had yet to be considered, while transport was still driven by animal and wind power.

Captain James Cook was sailing and searching for the supposed great southern land and he had just documented New Zealand.

It was into this world, permeated by superstitions and deep religious belief that Ann arrived. Her parents, James and Ann organised her baptism for the 1st of October 1769. The event is recorded in the church registers of both St Julian's[6] and St Etheldred's[7] which were only a short walk apart. It raises a curious question as to whether this is simply a clerical duplication, or was she in fact baptised twice on the same day? Both churches were also constructed using the local flint, which in the case of St Julian's, was a random mixture of brown, grey and white stones.

Figure 3: St Julian's Church[8]

ST JULIAN.

[4] Griffiths, Tom. n.d. *Artist's Impression of the Norwich City Walls on Their Completion in 1343.* Aviva Group Archive.
[5] Beresford. John 1924. *The Diary Of A Country Parson.* 9. http://archive.org/details/in.ernet.dli.2015.227134.
[6] 'Norfolk, England, Church of England Baptism, Marriages, and Burials, 1535-1812 for Ann Jarmy 1769, Norfolk, Norwich, St Julian. 1723-1803. Image 64'. n.d. Ancestry. Accessed 19 April 2023. https://www. ancestry.com.au
[7] 'Norfolk, England, Church of England Baptism, Marriages, and Burials, 1535-1812, Ann Jarmy 1769. Norfolk, Norwich, St Etheldreda. 1700-1781. Image 54'. n.d. Ancestry. Accessed 19 April 2023. https://www. ancestry.com.au
[8] Sillet, James. 1828. *Views of the Churches, Chapels, and Other Public Edifices in ... Norwich.* 47. https://play.google.com/books/reader?id=OusHAAAAQAAJ&pg=GBS.PA1771&hl=en.

Figure 4: St Etheldred's Church[9]

Ann was two years old when Captain Cook returned to England with news of his discovery of New Holland (Australia). She also became a big sister with the birth of her brother James.[10]

Early in 1772, on the other side of Norwich, another baby was entering the world. The little boy was destined to cross paths with Ann many years later. His name was Bishop Thompson. His parents Andrew and Ann had him baptised soon after his birth at the salt and pepper looking, flint stoned, St Giles' church.[11] [12]

Figure 5: Saint Giles Church.[13]

[9] Ibid, 29.
[10] 'Norfolk, England, Church of England Baptism, Marriages, and Burials, 1535-1812 for James Jarmy, Norfolk, Norwich, St Etheldreda. 1700-1781. Image 54'. 1771. Ancestry. 1771. https://www.ancestry.com.au.
'Norfolk, England, Church of England Baptism, Marriages, and Burials, 1535-1812 for Bishop Thompson 1772. Norfolk, Norwich, St Giles. 1757-1812. Image 32'. n.d. Ancestry. Accessed 19 April 2023. https://www.ancestry.com.au.
[12] 'Norfolk, England, Transcripts of Church of England Baptism, Marriage and Burial Registers, 1600-1935 for Bishop Thompson.
acon Transcripts 1600-1812, Norwich City Parishes. Image 25'. 1771. Ancestry. 1771. https://www.ancestry.com.au.
by the author Lisa Apfel. Taken 4th of July 2017.

The Norfolk Chronicle newspaper kept residents informed, reporting in 1775 about skirmishes over taxation erupting in the American colonies. Thomas Paine, a Norfolk man working in Philadelphia, used his position at the *Pennsylvania Magazine* to advocate for American independence in his influential pamphlet titled *Common Sense* which stated: "nothing can settle our affairs so expeditiously as an open and determined Declaration for Independence."[14]

It quickly gained traction, selling over half a million copies, and uniting the American people in their quest for independence.

Six months later, on the 4th of July 1776, they did declare their independence. A move that Britain refused to recognise so the battles continued for the resource rich colonies in what was the American War of Independence. Britain appeared to be getting the upper hand and Washington's army was in retreat by the end of the year and losing motivation. Paine wrote and published *Crisis 1* which Washington ordered to be read to his men at Valley Forge. It began with the now famous words: "These are the times that try men's souls."[15] The words were attributed with providing the motivation the troops needed.

In Norwich sympathies for the American rebels were high. A meeting was held in the Maid's Head hotel to try and garner donations to fight the rebels but "The Norfolk men...[had] so many relatives and friends among these same rebels, and so little love for King George, that they decided to refuse the government any pecuniary assistance."[16]

The supporters of the American revolution also produced propaganda which appealed to the illiterate masses such as Ann's family. What Ann's father, James, thought is unknown, but Ann's young mind may have been influenced. Evidence of her association with a Thomas Paine supporter later in her life has been found.[17] An example of the propaganda was the image in Figure 7 that combines the royal cypher GR with a rat. The implication being that King George was a rat.

At the start of 1778 Ann's sister Diana was born.[18]

[14] Paine, Thomas. 1945. *The Complete Writings of Thomas Paine*. Edited by Philip S. Foner. New York: Citadel Press. 38-39. http://archive.org/details/TheCompleteWritings.
[15] Ibid. 50.
[16] Tozier, Josephine. 1904. *Among English Inns: The Story of a Pilgrimage to Characteristic Spots of Rural England*. Boston: L. C. Page & Company. 212. https://link.gale.com/apps/doc/CYJJMG495400815/NCCO?sid=bookmark-NCCO&xid=b387a69d&pg=251.
[17] See page 28
[18] 'Norfolk, England, Church of England Baptism, Marriages, and Burials, 1535-1812 for Ann Jarmy, Norfolk, Norwich, St Etheldreda. 1700-1781. Image 54.' 1778. Ancestry. 1778. https://www.ancestry.com.au.

Figure 6: King George the Rat[19]

[19] '16925; Original Letters from Various Writers, Relating to the "Association for Preserving Liberty and Property against Republicans and Levellers," Addressed to John Reeves, Chairman, and John Moore, Secretary, between 2 November 1792, and 26 February,1793'. 1792. *Radicalism, Anti-Radicalism and Reform in England, 1769-1861: Original Papers and Minute Books: Original Papers and Minute Books from the Additional Manuscripts in the British Library*, November. 180. https://link.gale.com/apps/doc/BUXIAX549423519/GDCS?sid=bookmark-GDCS&xid=242b0a44&pg=180.

CHAPTER 2
NORWICH CONVICTIONS

"[On] the Tuesday before Midsummer Day,"[20] Ann and the other children of Norwich watched the annual Guild Day procession every year. It was held to celebrate the Lord Mayor's swearing-in ceremony and drew crowds to the streets and the marketplace. Colourful flags fluttered from windows. musicians played, and the cheering crowd celebrated. Ann and the other Norwich children would have been disappointed in 1881 when an evening storm delayed the planned fireworks until late at night.

Crime reports filled the newspapers, painting a grim picture of a society. People were hanged "for divers (sic) misdemeanours,"[21] including "house breaking, highway, and other robberies."[22]

Travelling on the roads was a perilous endeavour, with the constant threat of being held up at gunpoint or even murdered. Coaches travelling to London had to employ guards to reassure passengers.[23]

In February 1783, unbeknownst to Ann, a case emerged that would have consequences for her in later life.

> Some villains broke into the house of Mrs. Hambling, at Alburgh,
> near Harleston, in this county, and during the absence of the family,
> who were in the city, stripped it of every moveable, took the hangings
> from the bedsteads, and even the meat out of the pickle calks: it is
> supposed they also regaled themselves with wine, having left several
> empty bottles behind them.[24]

The culprits Abraham Carmen, Henry Cabell Snr and his son Henry Cabell Jnr were caught and sentenced to death. Sent to Norwich Castle, Henry the younger's sentence was later commuted to seven years transportation beyond the seas. He had to endure the horror of listening from his cell as his father was taken to the gallows on the 5th of April.

Nearly eight-and-a-half years after the American declaration of independence, Britain conceded defeat, which had significant ramifications for Britain. One of those consequences was Britain losing its ability to transport prisoners offshore.[25] Henry Cable found himself in limbo, and the French, who had aided the Americans in their fight for independence, took notice. One French observer said: 'May this

---

[20] The History and Antiquities of the County of Norfolk. 1781. 220.
[21] Beresford, John. The Diary Of A Country Parson. 248.
[22] *Norfolk Chronicle*. 1779. 'Home News', 20 March 1779. The British Newspaper Archive. 4.
https://www.britishnewspaperarchive.co.uk/viewer/bl/0000246/17790320/004/0002.
[23] *Norfolk Chronicle*. 1787. 'London and Norwich Expedition', 12 May 1787. The British Newspaper Archive. 3.
https://www.britishnewspaperarchive.co.uk/viewer/BL/0000246/17870512/013/0003?browse=true.
[24] *Norfolk Chronicle*. 1783. 'Home News', 8 February 1783. The British Newspaper Archive. 2.
https://www.britishnewspaperarchive.co.uk/viewer/bl/0000246/17830208/004/0002.
[25] The National Archives. n.d. 'How to Look for Records of...Criminal Transportation'. The National Archives. The National Archives.
Accessed 19 April 2023. https://www.nationalarchives.gov.uk/help-with-your-research/research-guides/criminal-transportation/.

great monument, raised to Liberty, serve as a lesson to the oppressor, and an example to the oppressed![26]

As a result of the loss of offshore transportation capabilities, prisons quickly became overcrowded, leading the government to employ decommissioned ships, known as prison hulks, to house prisoners. These ships, dilapidated, cold and leaky, were anchored in ports and rivers across the country. Recognising the need for a more permanent solution, word came from London in September 1786 that a convict settlement on the east coast of New Holland was to be established and Captain Arthur Phillip of the Royal Navy was commissioned as the Governor of the new colony. Newspapers reported that: "680 men felons and 70 women felons to go, who are to be guarded by 12 marines and a corporal in every transport containing 150 felons."[27]

They also reported that the convicts to go to Botany Bay would be made up of female convicts from London and male convicts from county gaols.[28] The hope being that the county convicts who were primarily from rural areas would have the skills in agriculture needed to start the new settlement.

The actual composition of convicts differed from this plan. Three women from Norwich Gaol were sent to Plymouth in preparation for the journey. The Norfolk Chronicle provided detailed coverage of their departure. One of the women, Susannah Holmes, had spent over two years in the gaol and had a child with Henry Cable.

> [W]hen the order came down for her removal [from the gaol] the man [Henry] was much distressed...application was made to the minister to permit him to go. [The application was denied and] the miserable woman was therefore obliged to go without the man...The child however was still her property, as the laws of England, which are distinguished by the spirit of humanity which framed them, forbid so cruel an act as that of separating an infant from its mother's breast. When Mr Simpson [the Norwich Gaoler] arrived at Plymouth with his party, he found they were to be put on board a hulk.[29]

Arriving at the hulk the captain refused to let the child onboard because he had no orders to take it.

> Neither the entreaties of Mr Simpson, nor the poor wretch, could prevail upon the captain even to permit the babe to remain till instructions could be received from the minister. Simpson was therefore obliged to take the child, and the frantic mother was led to her cell, execrating the cruelty of the man whose care she was now placed, vowing to put an end to her life.[30]

[26] Paine, Thomas. The Complete Writings of Thomas Paine. 255.
[27] Derby Mercury. 1786. 'London, (Thursday) Sept. 14', 14 September 1786. The British Newspaper Archive. 1. https://www.britishnewspaperarchive.co.uk/viewer/bl/0000189/17860914/003/0001.
[28] Norfolk Chronicle. 1787. 'Friday's Post and Express.', 13 January 1787. The British Newspaper Archive. 2. https://www.britishnewspaperarchive.co.uk/viewer/bl/0000246/17870113/004/0002.
[29] Norfolk Chronicle. 1786. 'Friday's Post and Express.', 11 November 1786. The British Newspaper Archive. 2. https://www.britishnewspaperarchive.co.uk/viewer/bl/0000246/17861111/017/0002.
[30] Ibid

Simpson with no choice had to try and get permission from the minister, Lord Sydney who lived in London, over two hundred miles away. It would take days to get there. He arrived unannounced and was told he would not get to see him for several days. Simpson was not to be deterred. He waited, and eventually Lord Sydney came down the stairs and:

> *was greatly affected...and instantly promised that the child should be*
> *restored, commending, at the same time, Mr Simpson's spirit and*
> *humanity. Encouraged by this, he made a further appeal to his*
> *Lordship's humanity in behalf of the father of the child, which*
> *proved equally successful; for his Lordship ordered, that he should*
> *likewise be sent to Plymouth to accompany the child and its mother,*
> *directing at the same time that they should be married before they*
> *went on board.[31]*

When Simpson got back to Norwich he informed Henry Cabel and "the poor man, who is a fine healthy young fellow seemed very grateful."[32]

The three women and Henry Kable as he became known were Norwich's contribution to Australia's First Fleet. Henry and Susannah were married just two weeks after their arrival in Sydney Cove. They are also remembered for bringing the first civil law case in the colony.[33] A remarkable feat in and of itself, however it was even more remarkable because they were still convicts and they were successful, being awarded fifteen pounds in damages.

Back in Norwich life was proving to be incredibly hard for Ann's parents, who were labelled as paupers. Ann's mother gave birth to another son who was named James just like Ann's first brother. This probably indicates that the first baby boy born in 1771 had died. The local minister gave the baby a private baptism even though they could not pay anything.[34] With the family in such a dire economic situation Ann who was nineteen, would have been out working.

Times were hard for many residents and one particular shop was attracting more than its fair share of thieves. Linen drapers, Lewis and Hayward, sold fine fabrics to the public. Located in the historic Norwich Market, their shop was located between two coffee houses. The other businesses nearby included a hatter and hosiery shop, a goldsmith and jeweller, an ironmonger, a woolen draper and a milliner.[35] The fabrics at Lewis and Hayward's would have appeared to be easy to take and easy to hide. The first thief caught was William Allen,[36] who was followed by Mary Bunn, then Elizabeth Allen and lastly Ann Jarmy.

William Allen was apprehended in July 1787. Caught stealing some handkerchiefs he was found guilty[37] [38] and sentenced to seven years

[31] Ibid
[32] Ibid
[33] Cable v. Sinclair [1788] NSWKR 7; [1788] NSWSupC 7.
[34] 'Norfolk, England, Church of England Baptism, Marriages, and Burials, 1535-1812 for James Jarmy 1788, Norwich, St Julian, 1770-1853. Image 7.' n.d. Ancestry. Accessed 19 October 2023. https://www. ancestry.com.au.
[35] Chase, William. 1783. *The Norwich Directory.* Norwich: W. Chase and Co. https://www.gutenberg.org/files/62333/62333-h/62333-h.htm.
[36] *The World.* 1792. 'Advertisements and Notices', 2 July 1792. Seventeenth and Eighteenth Century Burney Newspapers Collection. 3. https://link-gale-com.rp.nla.gov.au/apps/doc/Z2001536624/BBCN?u=nla&sid=bookmark-BBCN&xid=d2dbc6e5.
[37] *Norfolk Chronicle.* 1792. 'Bankrupts', 7 July 1792. British Library Newspapers.4. https://link-gale-com.rp.nla.gov.au/apps/doc/GR3218763291/BNCN?u=nla&sid=bookmark-BNCN&xid=3c892d27.
[38] *Norfolk Chronicle.* 1787. 'Home News', 4 August 1787. British Library Newspapers. https://link.gale.com/apps/doc/GR3218759003/BNCN?sid=bookmark-BNCN&xid=8f3d4572.

transportation.[39] He and two other Norwich prisoners, Robert Murrell and Peter Larkham were taken from Norwich to a prison hulk where they remained for over twelve months until the time came to board their ship to Sydney Cove. That ship was the *Scarborough (2)* and it was part of the Second Fleet, later known as the 'death fleet'. The conditions that the convicts experienced were described by William Hill:

> [T]he Villainy, oppression and shameful Peculation of the masters of
> the Transports [led to the misery]. - The Bark I was on board of, was
> indeed, unfit, from her make & size, to be sent to so great a
> Distance; if it blew but a trifling Gale, she was Lost in the Waters; of
> which she shipp'd so much, that from the Cape, the unhappy
> Wretches, the Convicts, were considerably above their waists in
> Water; and the men of my Company, whose Births were not so far
> forward, were nearly up to their middles; in this situation they were
> obliged, for the safety of the Ship, to be pen'd down; but when the
> Gales abated, no means were used to purify the air by Fumigations,
> no vinegar was applied, to rectify the nauseous steams, issuing from
> their miserable Dungeons; Humanity shudders to think that of nine
> hundred male Convicts embark'd in this Fleet, three Hundred and
> seventy are already Dead, & four hundred & fifty are landed sick,
> and so emaciated and helpless, that very few, or any of them, can be
> saved by care or medecine (sic); so that sooner it pleases God to
> remove them, the Better it will be for this Colony; which is not in a
> situation to bear any Burthen; as I imagine the Medicine Chest to be
> nearly exhausted and Provisions are a scarce Article.
> The irons used upon these unhappy Wretches were barbarous ; The
> Contractors had been in the Guinea Trade [slave trade] and had put
> on board the same Shackles, used by them in that Trade, which are
> made with a short Bolt, instead of Chains, that drop between the
> Legs and fasten with a Bandage about the Waist...these Bolts were
> not more than three Quarters of a Foot in Length so that they could
> not extend either Leg from the other, more than an inch or two at
> most ; Thus fettered it was impossible for them to move, but at the
> risque (sic) of both their Legs being broken...to this they were
> consigned, as well as a miserable Pittance of Provisions ; altho' the
> Allowance from Government is ample ; Even when attacked by
> Disease, their Situations were not altered, neither had they any
> Comforts administered ; the Slave Trade is mercifull (sic), compared
> to what I have seen in this Fleet ; in that it is the Interest of the
> Master to preserve the Health, & Lives of their Captives ; they
> having a joint Benefit, with their Owners, in this, the more they can

[39] 'New South Wales, Australia, Convict Indents, 1788-1842 for William Allen. List of Convict Transports, 1790-1791 (Second Fleet and Part of Third Fleet)'. n.d. Ancestry. Accessed 20 April 2023. Image 5. https://www. ancestry.com.au.

withhold from the unhappy Wretches, the more Provisions they have to [sell on arrival].[40]

Reverend Richard Johnson, also recorded what he saw:
I beheld a sight truly shocking to the feelings of humanity, a great number of them laying, some half, others nearly quite naked, without either bed or bedding, unable to turn or help themselves. Spoke to them as I passed along, but the smell was so offensive that I could scarcely bear it.... The landing of these people was truly affecting and shocking; great numbers were not able to walk, nor to move hand or foot; such were slung over the ship side in the same manner as they would a cask, a box, or anything of that nature. Upon their being brought up to the open air some fainted, some died upon deck, and others in the boat before they reached the shore. When come on shore many were not able to walk, to stand, or stir themselves in the least, hence some were led by others. Some creeped upon their hands and knees, and some were carried upon the backs of others.[41]

The unnamed *Lady Juliana* convict whose letter appeared in the Morning Chronicle gave another poignant account:

Oh! If you had but seen the shocking sight of the poor creatures that came out in the three ships it would make your heart bleed they were almost dead, very few could stand, and they were obliged to fling them as you would goods, and hoist them out of the ships, they were so feeble; and they died ten or twelve a day when they first landed; but some of them are getting better ... They were not so long as we were in coming here, but they were confined, and had bad victuals and stinking water. The Governor was very angry, and scolded the captains a great deal, and, I heard, intended to write to London about it, for I heard him say it was murdering them. It, to be sure, was a melancholy sight. What a difference between us and them.[42]

Robert Murrell was one of the convicts who died as the ship landed.[43] William Allen and Peter Larkham both survived and would have spent months regaining their strength.

Before William left for Sydney Cove, Mary Bunn was caught stealing from Lewis and Hayward. She was very fortunate to be acquitted of the charge because she was pregnant. The newspaper reported that:

[T]he wife of a respectable farmer, was tried for stealing four remnants of printed cotton out of the shop of Messrs. Lewis and Hayward. This was a cause of a very extraordinary nature, the facts being proved; but the defence set up was, that the prisoner, who was pregnant, conceived an irresistible longing for the goods in question,

[40] Wathen, Jonathan. 1790. 'Jonathan Wathen - Letter Received from William Hill, Sydney Cove, Port Jackson, 26 July 1790 (Copy Made in 1791)', 1791 1790. State Library of New South Wales. https://collection.sl.nsw.gov.au/record/9yMWVyx9.
[41] Bladen, F.M., ed. 1892. *Historical Records of New South Wales (1783-1792).* Vol. 1, Part 2. Sydney: Charles Potter, Government Printer. https://nla.gov.au/nla.obj-343658027.
[42] Flynn, Michael. 2016. 'Second Fleet'. The Dictionary of Sydney. 2016. https://dictionaryofsydney.org/entry/second_fleet.
[43] Smee, C J. 1790. 'Dr C J Smee's Early Colonial Australian 1788-1830 Database. Entry for Burial of Robert Murrell'. Fellowship of First Fleeters. 1790. http://www.fellowshipfirstfleeters.org.au/cjsmee_database/deadm_1.htm.

*and the jury having sufficient faith in this evidence, brought in their
verdict not guilty.*[44]

Two months later Ann, made the fateful decision to visit Lewis and Hayward's shop. Her arrest was reported in two papers:

*Wednesday last was committed the city gaol by Charles Weston Esq.
Mayor, Ann Jermey, charged upon the oath of William Rye, shopman
to Mess. Lewis and Hayward, linen drapers, in the Market-place
with privately stealing from out of their shop a remnant of printed
cotton cloth, containing four yards three quarters. Upon the
appearance of the constable, after she was detected, she attempted to
cut her throat, but was prevented.*[45]

And

*The present culprit exhibits no appearance of a longing condition,
which operated to acquit a former prisoner, in that state, for a
robbery in the same shop.*[46]

As the paper predicted, without a defence, like Mary Bunn, twenty-year-old Ann was destined to wait in the cell in the bowels of the Guildhall until her trial.

Her family's dire situation was the driving force behind the theft, but her response to being caught was a desperate and despairing act. Threating to cut her own throat showed her desperation and despair.

The cells under the floor of the Guildhall were windowless, small and devoid of any stimulation. It was a grim place for anyone, but for someone whose mental health was questionable, it would have been disastrous.

In the City Gaol she was under the watchful eye of Edward Sharp the gaol keeper.[47]She was also ministered to by reverend Buckle the chaplain of the gaol and for any medical emergencies James Keymer, the surgeon of the gaol would have attended.[48]

After three months in the gaol, she heard the footsteps as two more prisoners were brought down to the cells. "Bishop Thompson and Charles Barwick charged with stealing five spotted silk handkerchiefs, the property of Ann and Margaret Sargent, in St Andrew's."[49] Then two months later, another set of footsteps echoed through the halls. The irresistible fabrics of Lewis and Hayward's had tempted another. "Elizabeth Allen, charged on the oath of Mr. James Hayward, of St Peter's Mancroft, with privately stealing a remnant of purple and white printed cotton linen cloth, containing ten yards in length."[50]

[44] *Whitehall Evening Post (1770).* 1789. 'News', 1 September 1789. Seventeenth and Eighteenth Century Burney Newspapers Collection. 3. https://link-gale-com.rp.nla.gov.au/apps/doc/Z2001627485/BBCN?u=nla&sid=bookmark-BBCN&xid=3fd14e6a.
[45] *Norfolk Chronicle.* 1789. 'Home News', 22 August 1789. British Library Newspapers. 2. https://link-gale-com.rp.nla.gov.au/apps/doc/GR3218760764/BNCN?u=nla&sid=bookmark-BNCN&xid=c75d8484.
[46] *Northampton Mercury.* 1789. 'Wednesday & Thursday's Posts', 5 September 1789. British Library Newspapers. 2. https://link-gale-com.rp.nla.gov.au/apps/doc/GR3218880687/BNCN?u=nla&sid=bookmark-BNCN&xid=067a5d12.
[47] '1788, and 1789, January to August'. 1789. *Home Office Papers and Records: Part One: HO 42, Boxes 14, 1782-1792.* 321-322. https://link.gale.com/apps/doc/ALQWZC956572888/NCCO?u=nla&sid=bookmark-NCCO&xid=28255695.
[48] Ibid, 318.
[49] *Norfolk Chronicle.* 1789. 'Friday's Post', 14 November 1789. British Library Newspapers. 2. https://link-gale-com.rp.nla.gov.au/apps/doc/GR3218760942/BNCN?u=nla&sid=bookmark-BNCN&xid=ff3a48b1.
[50] *Norfolk Chronicle.* 1790. 'Friday's Post', 20 February 1790. British Library Newspapers. 2. https://link-gale-com.rp.nla.gov.au/apps/doc/GR3218761182/BNCN?u=nla&sid=bookmark-BNCN&xid=f6b89f35.

Elizabeth was very probably William Allen's wife.[51] Heartbroken that her husband had been sentenced to be transported across the seas and distressed by the thought of never seeing him again she must have thought the best way to stay with him was to commit the same crime, from the same shop. William was still on board the prison hulk when she was caught.

As Ann, Bishop, Charles and Elizabeth awaited their trials, news arrived in the city of the French people's rebellion. Influenced by figures like Thomas Paine they were awakening to the prospect of a republican society and the abolishment of the monarchy. Thomas Paine himself was invited to France to provide guidance in crafting a constitution and a *Declaration of the Rights of Man and of the Citizen*. He witnessed the storming of The Bastille and, was given the key to the Bastille pass on to Washington as a memento showing that "the principles of America opened the Bastille."[52]

Back in England, the trials of Ann and the other prisoners in Norwich commenced. Bishop and Charles were the first to be called up. Their guilt was swiftly determined, and they watched as the magistrate donned the black cap, a grim indication of what was to come. The awful sentence of death was pronounced.[53]

Three days later, on the 29th of July 1790, Ann and Elizabeth faced their trials.[54] Ann had endured nearly twelve months of confinement in gaol, living in limbo. Day after day, her life was devoid of exercise, stimulation, or joy. Her day in court would at least have given her closure, finally knowing her fate. It turned out to be transportation for seven years. Elizabeth received the same sentence.[55]

Two days later the judges wrote a letter seeking a sentence reduction for Bishop and Charles. It was sent to the King, saying:

> *some favourable circumstances appearing on their behalf at their trials we reprieved them and humbly recommend them as proper objects of Your Majesty's Royal Mercy to be pardoned ...on condition of his being transported beyond the Seas for the term of seven years to such a place as your Majesty by the advice of your Privy Council shall think fit.[56]*

The reply from the Home Secretary William Grenville arrived six days later, saying:

> *His majesty has...been graciously pleased to extend his Royal Mercy to...Bishop Thompson and Chas. Barwick on condition of their being severally transported for the term of seven years for the Eastern*

[51] A marriage was recorded at St. Stephen's on February 28, 1786, for a matching couple. See ''Norfolk, England, Transcripts of Church of England Baptism, Marriage and Burial Registers, 1600-1935. Archdeacon Transcripts 1600-1812. Norwich City Parishes. Image 135, 1786 for William Allen and Elizabeth Curle'. n.d. Ancestry. Accessed 22 April 2023. https://www. ancestry.com.au.

[52] Paine, Thomas. The Complete Writings of Thomas Paine. Xxvii.

[53] *Stamford Mercury*. 1790. 'STAMFORD, Aug. 6', 6 August 1790. British Library Newspapers. https://link-gale-com.rp.nla.gov.au/apps/doc/JA3230593991/BNCN?u=nla&sid=bookmark-BNCN&xid=90759bb0.

[54] 'New South Wales, Australia, Convict Indents, 1788-1842 for Ann Jarmy. List of Convict Transports. 1790-1791 (Second Fleet and Part of Third Fleet). Image 30'. n.d. Ancestry. Accessed 22 April 2023. https://www.ancestry.com.au.

[55] *Norfolk Chronicle*. 1790. 'Home News', 31 July 1790. British Library Newspapers. https://link-gale-com.rp.nla.gov.au/apps/doc/GR3218761640/BNCN?u=nla&sid=bookmark-BNCN&xid=6dcf408b.

[56] The National Archives. 1790. 'England & Wales, Crime, Prisons & Punishment Browse, 1770-1935, HO47, Judges' Reports On Criminals 1784-1830 - Correspondence, Piece13.' Findmypast. 31 July 1790. Images 307-309. https://search.findmypast.co.uk/record/browse?id=TNA/CCC/HO47/013A/00308.

Coast of New South Wales or some one or other of the Islands
adjacent.[57]

With their sentences now known, all four prisoners could only wait in their cells until they were transferred to the transport ships.

In their prison cells, they received a basic diet and survived on meagre rations and supplies. The prison system allowed for additional provisions if payments were made to gaolers or keepers. On Christmas Day, Mr. C. Copping, a local grocer, donated two pounds of beef, bread, beer, and porter (dark beer) to the twenty-one prisoners held in the city gaol. The prisoners also received an anonymous cash donation that "afforded much relief."[58]

Ann endured six more months in that cell until the 30th of January, when she, Bishop, Elizabeth, and Charles were "conveyed from the city gaol to Portsmouth for Botany Bay."[59] The transport ship *Mary Ann*, receiving only female prisoners, was anchored in Blackwell on the Thames River. Onboard, Ann would have heard the commotion as each new group of women joined the ship. Elizabeth would have been overjoyed at the thought that she would see William again soon.

After two weeks, the *Mary Ann* sailed downstream to Woolwich, where "a piteous sight presented itself this morning, in removing the female convicts from Newgate to the waterside; some swearing, others crying; some singing, and one poor woman, with a young child at her breast."[60]

A large crowd had gathered to witness their embarkation.[61] The *Mary Ann* continued down the Thames to Gravesend where it set sail for Botany Bay on the 18th of February.[62]

Meanwhile, Bishop and Charles were placed onboard the *William and Ann*. It departed from Gravesend a few days after the *Mary Ann* and made a stop at Portsmouth, where it joined the *Atlantic* and the *Salamander* before making a final stop at Plymouth. On the 23rd of March, all three ships set sail with their full complement of convicts.[63]

As the Third Fleet embarked on its journey, the ripples caused by Thomas Paine's latest pamphlet, *Rights of Man*, began to spread. Within a few weeks, fifty thousand copies were circulating in three editions. The pamphlet:

> *has made converts of many persons who were before enemies to the*
> *[French] revolution...[and] Englishmen were quoting passages ...*
> *with as much fervor (sic) as Americans had once recited sections*
> *from Common Sense... and many even quoted him to urge*

[57] The National Archives. 1790. 'England & Wales, Crime, Prisons & Punishment Browse, 1770-1935, HO13, Correspondence And Warrants, Piece7.' Findmypast. 4 August 1790. Images 531-532.
https://search.findmypast.co.uk/record/browse?id=TNA/CCC/HO13/007/00531.
[58] *Norfolk Chronicle*. 1791. 'News', 1 January 1791. British Library Newspapers. 2. https://go-gale-com.rp.nla.gov.au/ps/navigateToIssue?volume=22&loadFormat=page&issueNumber=1040&userGroupName=nla&inPS=true&mCode=2FXF&prodId=BNCN&issueDate=117910101.
[59] *Norfolk Chronicle*. 1791. 'News', 5 February 1791. British Library Newspapers.2. https://link-gale-com.rp.nla.gov.au/apps/doc/GR3218762074/BNCN?u=nla&sid=bookmark-BNCN&xid=6af8fba4.
60 Bath Chronicle and Weekly Gazette. 1791. 'London, Monday Feb. 14', 17 February 1791. The British Newspaper Archive. 2.
https://www.britishnewspaperarchive.co.uk/viewer/bl/0000221/17910217/007/0002.
[61] *Hereford Journal*. 1791. 'Tuesday & Wednesday's Posts', 16 February 1791. The British Newspaper Archive. 3.
https://www.britishnewspaperarchive.co.uk/viewer/bl/0000397/17910216/007/0003.
[62] *Ipswich Journal*. 1791. 'Friday's Post', 26 February 1791. The British Newspaper Archive. 2.
https://www.britishnewspaperarchive.co.uk/viewer/bl/0000191/17910226/005/0002.
[63] *Caledonian Mercury*. 1791. 'Plymouth March 24', 31 March 1791. The British Newspaper Archive. 3.
https://www.britishnewspaperarchive.co.uk/viewer/bl/0000045/17910331/012/0003.

Englishmen to follow the example set by their brothers across the channel.[64]

The English government viewed the pamphlet as seditious, and booksellers faced fines for selling it.[65]

Back in Sydney William Allen had made a complete recovery after the horrendous journey out. His skill as a mariner[66] had caught the attention of two convicts from the First Fleet, William and Mary Bryant. The couple were planning to escape the famine-stricken colony and sought skilled individuals like William Allen to aid them.

The Bryants had been married on the same day as Henry and Susannah Kable, and now had a toddler and a newborn baby. They were resolute in their decision to leave Botany Bay.

William Bryant set his plan in motion when a sympathetic Dutch captain arrived in the harbour. He acquired a six-oared[67] fishing boat and other necessary supplies from the captain.[68] When the Dutch captain sailed his ship out of Sydney Cove on the 28th of March,[69] William Bryant signalled his six recruits, including William Allen, that it was time to act. Under the cover of darkness that night, they loaded their supplies of rice, flour, salted pork, and navigation tools into the boat and pushed off.

William Allen was no doubt hopeful about being reunited with Elizabeth back in Norwich, never dreaming that she had departed England just five days before and was on her way to Botany Bay.

The boat "with an old lug [sail], main sail and fore-sail, but without any covering"[70] provided no protection against the elements. It leaked and required constant repairs. The exposure to the wind, rain and sun was relentless.

Their plan was to reach Koepang in Timor, over 1,300 miles away,[71] where they hoped to find refuge in the Dutch colony.

---

[64]Paine, Thomas. The Complete Writings of Thomas Paine. Xxviii.

[65] 'ENGLAND AND WALES: Miscellaneous: Petition of George Robinson et al, Booksellers, Asking...' 1796. The National Archives. 2 March 1796. https://discovery.nationalarchives.gov.uk/details/r/C7666693.

[66] Causer, Tim, ed. 2017. *Memorandoms by James Martin. An Astonishing Escape from Early New South Wales.* London: UCL Press. 18. https://discovery.ucl.ac.uk/id/eprint/1558725/1/Memorandoms-by-James-Martin.pdf.

[67] Martin, James. 1794. 'Memorandom by James Martin Box 169 Folio 179-201'. Bentham Papers Database. Folio 180. http://transcribe-bentham.ucl.ac.uk/td/JB/169/180/001.

[68] Collins, David. 1804. *An Account of the English Colony in New South Wales, from Its First Settlement in January 1788 to August 1801.* 2d edition. Vol. 1. London: Cadell & Davies. 129. https://www.biodiversitylibrary.org/item/172462.

[69] Ibid. 128.

[70] *The World.* 1792. 'Advertisements and Notices', 2 July 1792. Seventeenth and Eighteenth Century Burney Newspapers Collection. 3. https://link-gale-com.rp.nla.gov.au/apps/doc/Z2001536624/BBCN?u=nla&sid=bookmark-BBCN&xid=d2dbc6e5.

[71] Ibid.

Figure 7: Coupang, Timor.[72]

The small group made frequent stops for repairs and to gather fresh water. Mary, who was breastfeeding, needed water to sustain her milk production. They searched for suitable camping spots along the shorelines while remaining cautious of potential attacks from local Aboriginal people. Their only defence was to fire their gun as a warning, hoping to scare away any potential attackers.

As they continued, the boat began to sit lower in the water, raising their concerns that it would be swamped. In an effort to lighten the load, they threw their spare clothes overboard.

Against all the odds, "the poor creatures"[73] arrived in Timor after more than two months and presented themselves to the colony's governor as shipwreck survivors, however, their ruse did not last. The Dutch Governor "discovered, by overhearing their conversation, to have been convicts at Botany Bay, and to have escaped from thence."[74]

Captain Edward Edwards commanding the wrecked ship *Pandora* arrived in Timor with his surviving crew and the mutineers he had captured from the *Bounty*. The escaped convicts were handed over to him to take back to England. Only half of them survived the journey. Despite being fifty-five years old[75], William Allen, considered an old man, was among the survivors. He and the other survivors were taken to London, where they were "to remain in prison until their original sentence of transportation is expired."[76]

---

[72] Lesueur, Charles Alexandre. 1807. *Timor, Vue de La Rade, de La Ville et Du Fort de Coupang (Kupang)*. Engraving. National Library of Australia. https://nla.gov.au/nla.obj-150874947.
[73] Ibid.
[74] Ibid.
[75] Causer, Tim, ed. Memorandoms by James Martin. An Astonishing Escape from Early New South Wales. 18.
[76] *Derby Mercury*. 1792. 'London', 12 July 1792. The British Newspaper Archive. https://www.britishnewspaperarchive.co.uk/viewer/bl/0000052/17920712/017/0004.

CHAPTER 3

ARRIVAL AT THE CONVICT COLONY

The French built whaling vessel, *Mary Ann*,[77]that Ann boarded, had been actively engaged in whaling operations for the previous few years before returning in preparation for its new role transporting convicts. To safeguard the ship's hull from the destructive, timber boring naval shipworm, it was copper lined. The *Mary Ann* also carried whaleboats that were deployed in the hunt.

Whaling was described as:

> one of the largest, most profitable, and important businesses of the day, involving tens of thousands of workers at sea and on shore, and millions of dollars in annual investments and returns...[It is needed to] supply the rapidly industrializing Western world with oil for its lamps, candles, and machinery, and baleen for its parasol ribs, horsewhips, and corsets.[78]

Under the contract of Messrs. Camden, Calvert, and King (Calvert & Co.), the Commissioners of the Navy entrusted the responsibility of supplying all the fleet's ships. [79] Thirty-year-old Captain Mark Munro [80] was appointed to command the *Mary Ann*, while Captain Eber Bunker assumed command of the *William and Ann*.

The *Mary Ann's* ocean bound community consisted of 142 women, six children,[81] the captain and the crew. They were the second load of purely female prisoners following on from the *Lady Juliana* of the Second Fleet. The women aboard the *Lady Juliana* discovered that by living as the 'wives' of the crew they could secure "better provisions and sleeping arrangements."[82] Having endured months or even years of meagre rations and confinement in small, cramped, and dismal prison spaces, these women seized the opportunity to improve their circumstances. Women aboard the *Mary Ann* also sought to enhance their lives by forming relationships with the crew. Ann started a serious relationship with Thomas Tambleton,[83] while Captain Munro found a partner in Ann Carey from Bristol.

[77] Lloyd's Register Foundation, Heritage & Education Centre. 1792. *Lloyd's Register of Shipping 1792.* http://archive.org/details/HECROS1792.

[78] Williford, James. 2010. 'Whaling The Old Way'. *Humanities the Magazine of The National Endowment for the Humanities*, April 2010. https://www.neh.gov/humanities/2010/marchapril/feature/whaling-the-old-way.

[79] Bladen. Historical Records of New South Wales. Vol. 1, Part 2. 463.

[80] 'Devonshire Street Cemetery, Sydney for Mark Monro Death Date 18 Jun 1821.' 2021. Project Gutenberg Australia. 2021. http://gutenberg.net.au/Devonshire-street/people/PersonPN14622.html..

[81] Collins. An Account of the English Colony in New South Wales. 137.

[82] Lewis, Robert. 2009. 'Study Guide: The Floating Brothel. A Dramatised Documentary'. National Film and Sound Archive of Australia. 2009. https://www.nfsa.gov.au/sites/default/files/05-2017/floating_brothel_tn.pdf.

[83]Children were baptised with their mother's surname if the father was unknown, generally suggesting either non-consensual intercourse or promiscuous behaviour. Margaret Tambleton being baptised with her father's surname suggests that the relationship of Ann and Thomas was acknowledged.

Ann began her relationship with Thomas soon after sailing. After a month onboard she would have realised she was pregnant. The absence of her period would have been a blessing on board.

After a relatively quick four-month voyage, the women reached Botany Bay on the 9th of July 1791, with only a single stop of ten days at St Jago.[84] It took an additional six weeks for the *William and Ann* to arrive, and the *Admiral Barrington* was the final vessel of the fleet to join them.

As the women disembarked, David Collins, the Judge Advocate, remarked that they appeared "healthy."[85] Ann was assigned a hut constructed from the wood of the cabbage tree,[86] chosen for its straight trunks ideal for building sturdy walls. The convicts' and officers' huts were arranged around the Cove and The Rocks "without any kind of regularity."[87]

Figure 8: Cabbage Tree Forest[88]

[84] Collins. An Account of the English Colony in New South Wales. 138.
[85] Ibid
[86] Harris, John. 1791. 'John Harris - Papers, 1791-1837', 20 March 1791. State Library of New South Wales. 2. https://collection.sl.nsw.gov.au/record/Yj7dzlD9/mrLAKQKMb4O0x.
[87] Ibid. 3.
[88] Earle, Augustus. 1827. *Cabbage Tree Forest, Illawarra, New South Wales*. Watercolour. National Library of Australia. https://nla.gov.au/nla.obj-134499059.

Ann arrived at a growing and developing society that contained many ex-convicts who had completed their sentences. Governor Phillip was guided by a core policy from England that ex-convicts were to become settlers and cultivate the land.[89] England didn't want them back so developed the idea that if they were given land the ex-convicts would want to stay. They were given small allotments of land, "30 acres for a man, 20 acres for a wife and 10 acres for each child. The seeds, tools and rations they needed to establish themselves."[90]

Just three months before Ann's arrival on the 30th of March 1791 the first of these emancipist settlers James Ruse was given the first land grant out at Parramatta.[91] The day also saw three other men get their land grants. Phillip Schaeffer the superintendent of convicts[92] with 140 acres and two marines who had agreed to become settlers rather than return to England, Robert Webb and William Reid, getting 60 acres.[93] Then nine days after Ann's arrival another twenty-three emancipist convicts followed in James Ruse's steps and were granted their lands near Parramatta. One of them was Charles Williams, who had also arrived onboard the *Scarborough* with Ruse[94] and was now his neighbour.[95]

The Parramatta population of over one hundred[96] people consisted of these settlers as well as convicts and soldiers.

Governor Phillip had plans to settle the Hawkesbury River area that he had sailed to in June 1789. He had seen the river flats that could be farmed but knew that the distance from Sydney was an issue. He had to find settlers that he could trust saying "before a settlement can be made there, proper people to conduct it must be found and we must be better acquainted with the country."[97]

The settlement at Sydney Cove was transitioning from the quickly constructed, rudimentary infrastructure and buildings put up after the First and Second Fleets to more permanent structures. Buildings such as Governor Phillip's house, David Collins' house, and the newly appointed Commissariat John Palmer's house, were all crafted from locally made bricks that were made at to the south of Sydney at Brickfields.

The government was facing significant struggles in providing food and clothing for the convicts. Multiple factors contributed to this predicament, including insufficient supplies arriving with the fleets, losses due to theft, rats, inadequate storage on the ships, failed crop harvests, unskilled labour and inadequate manufacturing facilities. In response, the *Atlantic* was dispatched to Calcutta in search of essential supplies.

On arrival Ann was put to work in the fields. The numbers of women helping to grow the colony's food had increased over the previous year as Governor Phillip realised, they had to be able to provide it for those who were incapable or employed

[89] Karskens, Grace. 2020. *People of the River*. Crows Nest, NSW: Allen & Unwin. 75.
[90] Ibid, 73.
[91] Fletcher, B. H. 1967. 'James Ruse (1759–1837)'. In *Australian Dictionary of Biography*. Vol. 2. Canberra: National Centre of Biography, Australian National University. https://adb.anu.edu.au/biography/ruse-james-2616.
[92] 'Colonial Secretary Index, 1788-1825 - Scarr, G to Schools (1820) for Phillip Schaffer'. n.d. MHNSW. Accessed 18 March 2024. https://colsec.records.nsw.gov.au/s/F50c_sa-sf-06.htm#P2825_83231.
[93] Bladen. Historical Records of New South Wales. Vol. 1, Part 2. 540.
[94] Tompkin, Erin, and John Boyd. 2009. 'Scarborough Convict Transport'. Fellowship of First Fleeters. 2009. http://www.fellowshipfirstfleeters.org.au/ship_scarborough.htm.
[95] Both were "eastern settlers" on exceedingly good ground. See Bladen, F.M., ed. 1892. *Historical Records of New South Wales (1783-1792)*. Vol. 1, Part 2. 599.
[96] Ibid, 299.
[97] Ibid, 350.

in other areas.[98] Married women attended their huts[99] and when fabrics became available some women were put to work making clothes.[100]

Thomas remained aboard, assisting with cargo unloading and preparing the ship for its next voyage, thus marking the end of his relationship with Ann. The *Mary Ann* set sail for Norfolk Island on the 8th of August, returning a month later. Upon its return, the crew, including Thomas, were required to stay on board unless they obtained a permit to disembark. The Governor had introduced the permit system in response to various crews bringing alcohol from the ships and supplying it to the convicts.

Having fulfilled the government contract, Captain Munro prepared the ship to go whaling. He and the captains of the *William and Ann, Matilda, Britannia*, and *Salamander* all had instructions to return to England fully laden with oil.[101]

On the 24th of October the *Mary Ann* and the *Matilda* sailed south on a sealing expedition whilst the *William and Ann* in company with the *Britannia* set out in search of whales.[102][103] The *Mary Ann* encountered a fierce storm that damaged two whaleboats and the blubber boiling pots used to extract oil. As a result, the ship was compelled to return to Sydney after two-and-a-half weeks for repairs. In the port the copper lined hull was thoroughly washed down in readiness to set off again.[104]

[98] Ibid, 359.
[99] Watson, Frederick, ed. 1914. *Historical Records of Australia (1788-1796)*. Vol. 1. 1. Sydney: Library Committee of the Commonwealth Parliament. 357. https://nla.gov.au/nla.obj-472896848.
[100] Tench, Watkin and Royal Australian Historical Society. 1979. Sydney's First Four Years : Being a Reprint of A Narrative of the Expedition to Botany Bay and, A Complete Account of the Settlement at Port Jackson / by Watkin Tench ; with an Introduction and Annotations by L.F. Fitzhardinge. Sydney: Library of Australian History in association with the Royal Australian Historical Society. 259
[101] Collins. An Account of the English Colony in New South Wales. 148.
[102] Bladen. Historical Records of New South Wales. Vol. 1, Part 2. 555-558.
[103] Hunter, John. 2005. *An Historical Journal of the Transactions at Port Jackson and Norfolk Island*. Project Gutenberg. https://www.gutenberg.org/ebooks/15662/pg15662-images.html.
[104] Watson. Historical Records of Australia. Vol. 1. 1. 307-308

Figure 9: Whaling[105]

[105] Downes, Henry William. 1846. *Illustrated Log of the Whaling Barque TERROR*. Object No 00038301. Australian National Maritime Museum. https://collections.sea.museum/en/objects/details/11429/.

Figure 10: Departure of the Whaler Britannia from Sydney Cove [106]

[106] Whitcombe, Thomas. 1798. *Departure of the Whaler Britannia from Sydney Cove*. Painting: oil on canvas. National Library of Australia. https://nla.gov.au/nla.obj-134108884.

As November arrived, the temperature soared to a scorching thirty-four degrees Celsius, leading to a reduction in convict work hours. The availability of fresh water grew increasingly scarce, prompting authorities to issue orders prohibiting the washing down of ships. Rations were also diminished during this challenging period.

Ann would never have felt temperatures like it in Norwich, nor would she have experienced such a scarcity of water. Her struggle to adapt would have been compounded by the fact that she was now seven months pregnant.

The *Mary Ann* embarked on another swift whaling voyage, returning with nine whales killed and thirty barrels of oil produced.[107] Then it sailed out of the colony for the final time, bound for Peru, taking Thomas with it.[108]

The world Ann found herself in was eloquently described by another convict, the artist Thomas Watling:

> *The vast number of green frogs, reptiles, and large insects, among the grass and on the trees, during the spring, summer, and fall, make an incessant noise and clamour. They cannot fail to surprise the stranger exceedingly, as he will hear their discordant croaking just by, and sometimes all around him, though he is unable to discover whence it proceeds:- nor can he perceive the animals from whence the sounds in the trees issue, they being most effectually hid among the leaves and branches...Birds, flowers, shrubs, and plants; of these, many are tinged with hues that must baffle the happiest efforts of the pencil. Quadrupeds are by no means various; but we have a variety of fishes, the greater part of which, are dropped and spangled with gold and silver, and stained with dyes transparent and brilliant as the arch of heaven... the whole appearance of nature must be striking in the extreme to the adventurer, and at first this will seem to him to be a country of enchantments. The generality of the birds and the beasts sleeping by day, and singing or catering in the night, is such an inversion in nature as is hitherto unknown...To see what has been done in the space of five or six years of clearing, building, and planting, is astonishing.[109]*

A month after Thomas's departure, Ann gave birth to their daughter on the 4th of January 1792. She was just twenty-two years old, alone and without any support or guidance. Caring for her newborn would have been a case of trial and error. Learning as she went. After eleven days she managed to arrange the baptism of baby Margaret Tambleton.[110][111]

[107] Collins. An Account of the English Colony in New South Wales. 154.
[108] *The Scots Magazine*. 1793. 'Account Of Capt. Bligh's Expedition To The South Seas', 1 February 1793. https://www.britishnewspaperarchive.co.uk/viewer/bl/0000545/17930201/016/0035.
[109] Watling, Thomas. 1794. 'Letters From An Exile At Botany Bay, To His Aunt In Dumfries'. The University of Sydney Australian Digital Collections. University of Sydney Library. 1794. https://adc.library.usyd.edu.au/view?docId=ozlit/xml-main-texts/p00061.xml&chunk.id=d1324e262&toc.id=d1324e147&database=&collection=&brand=default.
[110] 'Registers of Baptisms, Burials and Marriages, Series NRS 12937, Reel 5002, Baptism Margaret Tambleton V1792163 4'. 1792. Museums of History New South Wales - State Archives Collection.
[111] Mutch, T.D., and Genealogical Society of the Church of Jesus Christ of Latter-Day Saints. 1974. 'Mutch Card Indexes [Microform]'. Reel 2125: 1787-1814 from Abbott to Tillet. Margaret Tambleton Baptism and Burial'. Central West Libraries.

Figure 11: View of Sydney Cove by Thomas Watling [112]

[112] Watling, Thomas. 1794. *View of Sydney Cove*. Watercolour on paper. State Library of New South Wales.
https://collection.sl.nsw.gov.au/record/nmQdrexn/8OZkB2xgBwWa4

Tragedy struck when little Margaret passed away just two months later, deepening Ann's grief and solitude.[113] [114]

The colony itself was not faring any better. Governor Phillip expressed concern about the ongoing hardships, stating:

> the colony...still suffers from having been for such a length of time at
> a reduced ration... the inconveniences are felt, and people are
> dispirited...but little labour is done at present, for the people are in
> general very weak.[115]

Ann would have been put back to work in the fields after Margaret's death. Her working hours were reduced due to the starving state that all the agricultural workers were in. They laboured outdoors from 5 am to 9 am and again from 4 pm to 5:30 pm.[116]

As the *Atlantic* had not yet returned from Calcutta with the needed supplies, arrangements were made for the recently arrived ship *Pitt* to undertake the same journey. Its purpose was to procure provisions in case the *Atlantic* had "met with any accident in her passage."[117]

Amidst this grim landscape, the newly arrived commander of the New South Wales Corps, Major Grose, appeared and was impressed by the flourishing vegetable garden surrounding his house.[118] His view, was contradicted by longtime resident Collins who knew the grim reality. He observed:

> The mortality in the month of April had been extremely great.
> Distressing as it was, however, to see the poor wretches daily
> dropping into the grave, it was far more afflicting to observe the
> countenances and emaciated persons of many who remained, soon to
> follow their miserable companions...The weakest of the convicts
> were excused from all kinds of hard labour; but it was not hard
> labour that destroyed them; it was an entire want of strength in the
> constitution, and which nothing but proper nourishment could
> repair.[119]

Ann continued to live hand to mouth and day to day. Over the next eight months only the *Atlantic*, and the *Britannia* arrived, each arrival raising her hopes that the rationing would finally end, and the suffering would be over. Her hopes were repeatedly dashed.

As the colony expanded, so did its problems. Land cultivation efforts in Parramatta offered hope, of a good food supply but the harvested corn was picked and eaten by hungry convicts before it could get to the store.[120] The result was the introduction of night watch patrols.[121]

---

[113] Ibid.
[114] 'Registers of Baptisms, Burials and Marriages, Series NRS 12937, Reel 5002, Burial Margaret Tambleton V1792465 4'. 1792. Museums of History New South Wales - State Archives Collection.
[115] Bladen. Historical Records of New South Wales. Vol. 1, Part 2. 596-598.
[116] Ibid, 610-611.
[117] Ibid, 601.
[118] Ibid, 613.
[119] Collins. An Account of the English Colony in New South Wales. 167.
[120] Bladen. Historical Records of New South Wales. Vol. 1, Part 2. 644-645.
[121] 'New South Wales, Australia, Colonial Secretary's Papers, 1788-1856. Special Bundles, 1794-1825. Image 18016-18017 for 1789'. n.d. Ancestry. Accessed 28 May 2022. https://www.ancestry.com.au.

The night watch was an intriguing mix of convicts, in a unique position of policing soldiers and sailors. They "were promised to be rewarded in future if they were honest and vigilant [and] punished with the utmost rigor of the law, [for their negligence]."[122] The governor reported that the scheme was successful.[123]

Among the night watchmen, was Samuel Howell, a survivor of the death fleet, under a life sentence. He no doubt held onto hope that his reward would be a pardon. He had begun his night watch duties in about 1792.[124]

For Ann, being surrounded and outnumbered by men had its pros and cons. While it made her vulnerable to potential attacks, it also provided her with the opportunity to be discerning in choosing a permanent partner. The partner she chose was Samuel Howell.

---

[122] Ibid.
[123] Watson. Historical Records of Australia. Vol. 1. 1. 134
[124] Granted for his duty in the night watch for over eight years. See 'Samuel Howell- Conditional Pardon [4/4430]; Reel 774 p 012'. 1800. Museums of History New South Wales - State Archives Collection.

CHAPTER 4
AUTONOMY

One can easily imagine that Samuel's role in the night watch would have evoked both desire and disdain. For a convict, it liberated him from arduous government labour, giving him the energy and ability to work around his own hut in the day. It also placed him in a relatively powerful position. The soldiers must have looked at the situation as ludicrous. To have prisoners 'policing' soldiers!

Living as a couple, Ann was able to stop working in the fields and focus on working in her home and garden.

As summer arrived, she would have experienced scorching temperatures far in excess of anything she had felt before. On the 5th of December, the howling winds combined with the high temperatures to drive a bushfire through the grass at the back of the hill on the western side of the cove. Ann would have seen, smelt and probably feared the sight of it as it threatened the thatched huts. The choking smoke engulfed the surroundings. The blaze destroyed one house and several gardens and their fences.[125] The identity of those who lost their house, and gardens remains unknown, leaving the possibility that Ann and Samuel could have been among the victims.

Figure 12: A western view of Sydney Cove 1798[126]

---

[125] Ibid 195

[126] Dayes, Edward, and Thomas Watling. 1797. *[Western View of Sydney Cove, 1797]*. https://nla.gov.au/nla.obj-134426258.

Six days later, Governor Phillip boarded the *Atlantic*, setting sail for England due to his ailing health. Major Grose, the military leader, assumed the responsibility of governing the colony on the 11th of December 1792.

At 5:45 am on Sunday morning, before the heat of the day, the drums beat to summon the handful of faithful for mass. The service took place in the open air, as there was no church yet.[127] Like most convicts, Ann no longer attended religious services.[128]

On the eve of Christmas, the *Hope* arrived from America, selling its alcohol to the Commissary. This was followed by the arrival of the *Kitty* and *Bellona* early in the new year. Each arrival sparked hopes that the rationing would end, and each time the disappointment was palpable. Grose reassessed the situation and determined that his military personnel should not endure the same rationing as the convicts, and promptly ordered an increase in their wheat allowance.[129]

Furthermore, he began giving land grants to his officers and assigning convicts to work on their newly allocated private plots. This use of free labour bolstered the officers' properties and wealth but had adverse effects on government projects. The clearing of trees, ploughing, cultivation of private lands, and construction of houses were all conducted using this unpaid labour force.

Not only were food and clothes in short supply, so too was cash. Goods and services were paid for with "rum, sugar, tea and articles of this nature, money being of little use."[130]

Opposition to Grose's management soon surfaced. Chief amongst his opponents were the two ministers of the colony: Reverends Richard Johnson and Samuel Marsden. The latter writing that the police are:

> *very bad... Major G*r*. Grose,... [is] so very bad & licentious a*
> *character [and has] opened a door to all kinds of Immorality &*
> *Irreligions (sic) & Idleness, Drunkenness & Profaneness ...amongst*
> *the Convicts, [and also] all Ranks & Orders...The greatest Part of*
> *the Officers sold Spiritous Liquors, & enriched themselves at the*
> *Expense of the Morals of the People- The more Drunkenness, the*
> *more Money returned into their Pockets...the Convicts [have] full*
> *Liberty to absent themselves from divine Worships & permission to*
> *spend the Sabbath Day in any manner their Passions excited them.*[131]

Surgeon Arndell later commented that:

> *habitual drunkenness absolutely became the unfortunate fashion of*
> *the times ; the consequence was that crimes of every sort increased*
> *to an alarming degree ; thefts and robberies became so numerous*
> *that they were spoken of as mere matters of course, and even rapes*
> *and murders were not infrequent...The Sabbath...was profaned as a*

[127] Collins. An Account of the English Colony in New South Wales. 197.

[128] Assumption based on the fact that no baptisms of her children are recorded after Margaret Tambleton's.

[129] Collins. An Account of the English Colony in New South Wales. 192-193.

[130] 'Rev. Samuel Marsden (Sydney) to William Wilberforce (?) Papers of Archbishop John Moore (as Filmed by the AJCP)/File 4'. 1794, 4 May 1794. 4. Lambeth Palace Library. http://nla.gov.au/nla.obj-1370817647.

[131] Marsden, Samuel. 1796. 'S. Marsden (Parramatta) to [Unknown] (as Filmed by the AJCP) [Microform] : [M2686-M2696], 1795-1965./Fonds C 84/Series C 84/1', 16 September 1796. West Yorkshire Archive Service, Wakefield. http://nla.gov.au/nla.obj-1444999833.

day appropriated to gaming, intoxication, and the uncontrolled indulgence of every vicious excess. [132]

The balancing act of issuing supplies continued. The arrival of the *Dædalus* and the privately owned *Shah Hormzear* with their quality supplies was offset by the withered maize crop.

Convicts' work hours were increased to six hours of labour, five days a week. Still hungry, many resorted to raiding the fields for sustenance.

The winter of 1793 was "colder than any that they had yet experienced." [133] Convicts skilled in sewing were engaged in creating additional clothes and shoes for distribution. Ann, clad in threadbare garments and suffering from hunger, would have lined up to receive her allocation, however, her new clothes would not fit her for long, as she was pregnant once again.

The king's birthday was a day of celebration but more importantly for Ann and Samuel, a day off work. Held on the 4th of June each year, it was an excuse for many convicts to get drunk. They could "barter their supplies for spirits." [134] Meanwhile, the military and superintendents received an extra portion of pork as a gift from Grose. [135]

A week later, Ann's despair must have deepened upon hearing that Grose intended to reduce their rations unless supplies arrived soon. The subsequent arrival of the *Britannia* would have raised her hopes, but they were soon shattered when it was announced that the ship carried nothing for the convicts. Every animal disembarking and every container unloaded had been privately chartered by the officers of the New South Wales Corps for their own benefit. [136] Consequently, Ann's pork allowance was reduced.

Hopeful eyes eagerly scanned the horizon for relief in the form of rations, and the next ship to arrive was the *Boddingtons*. The cargo it brought was negated by the large number of Irish convicts onboard. The pattern repeated with the arrival of the *Sugar Cane* in September.

Out at Parramatta James Ruse and Charles Williams had decided that they had had enough of the colony and sold up their land grants. [137] Charles who was from London probably had no farming experience before his arrival and was in all likelihood eager to get back to the metropolis. [138][139] Both men started living off the profits of their land sales while waiting for a ship that would take them back and it wasn't long before they had exhausted their funds. [140]

As the ground warmed up the winter crop of wheat was ready to harvest. After harvesting, the ground was ploughed and planted with the summer crop of maize. The maize then ripened towards the end of summer and into autumn when the ears

[132] Bladen, F.M., ed. 1895. *Historical Records of New South Wales (1796-1799)*. Vol. 3. Sydney: Charles Potter, Government Printer. 437-438. https://nla.gov.au/nla.obj-359069148.
[133] Ibid, 219.
[134] Ibid, 218.
[135] Ibid, 214.
[136] Ibid, 181.
[137] Collins. An Account of the English Colony in New South Wales. 246.
[138] 'Trial of Charles Williams (T17840707-7)'. 1784. Old Bailey Proceeding Online. July 1784. https://www.oldbaileyonline.org/record/t17840707-7.
[139] National Centre of Biography, Australian National University. n.d. 'Charles Williams (1762-1815)'. People Australia. Accessed 16 March 2024. https://peopleaustralia.anu.edu.au/biography/williams-charles-29820/text36913.
[140] Collins. An Account of the English Colony in New South Wales. 231.

of maize were picked, the stems dug out and the ground replanted with wheat ready to start all over again.

The 1793 maize harvest was a poor one for the government, who hoped to supplement the stores with surplus grown by settlers. The government offered a low price of five shillings per bushel which the settlers mostly ignored. They could turn the maize into spirits which held a higher market value. They wanted labourers to work their farms and knew they could exchange the alcohol with convicts for their labour.[141]

It was common knowledge that the river flats on the Hawkesbury River were potentially the best farming land in the colony, but the problem as Governor Phillip had previously pointed out was that he knew little about the area and needed "proper people"[142] to set up the settlement. James Ruse and Charles Williams, now with colonial farming experience and no funds to return to England approached Grose to seek permission to settle the area. He agreed and the two men along with twenty others set off.[143] (See Figure 16). They found an open area that was clear of the surrounding "towering, tangled, squelching country,"[144]thanks to the fire management practices of the local Aboriginal people. They set about picking their land and sowing some maize. They marked trees for boundaries and set up small pens to fence their animals as well as building their huts to live in.

Ann and Samuel lived together as husband and wife, despite not being officially married, and in 1794, their happiness can be imagined as they welcomed their baby, Henry, into their family.[145][146] In England a mother recovering from childbirth was fed porridge made from oats. In the colony there were no oats, so Ann was fed a gruel made by boiling ground up maize and water.[147]

Critical shortages of food forced the government into buying meat from settlers to feed the military. Convicts like Ann and Samuel were facing the prospect of only being issued bread from the store. An untenable situation that forced them to consider slaughtering one of their breeding sows.[148]

In Sydney Cove, the supply ship *Indispensable* arrived just as the autumn air was cooling. It was followed by other supply ships in quick succession. These ship arrivals in conjunction with the completion of the local flour mill helped build up the government stores, until full rations were announced, in March 1794. A first since Ann's arrival.[149]

In the colony, Ann found herself seriously outnumbered. From a total white population of almost six thousand people, less than one thousand were women.[150] When Samuel was working the night watch, she would almost certainly have felt a sense of trepidation and vulnerability.

[141] Ibid, 224.
[142] Bladen. Historical Records of New South Wales. Vol. 1, Part 2. 350.
[143] Karskens. People of the River. 89.
[144] Ibid, 185.
[145] Aged 34 in '1828 New South Wales, Australia Census (Australian Copy) for Henry Howell. (NRS 1272)1828 Census: Alphabetical Return. Surnames C-L. Image 436'. n.d. Ancestry. Accessed 24 April 2023. https://www.ancestry.com.au.
[146] Aged 21 in 'Registers of Baptisms, Burials and Marriages, Series NRS 12937, Reel 5002, Marriage Henry Howell V1815 151 7'. 1815. Museums of History New South Wales - State Archives Collection.
[147] 'Rev. Samuel Marsden (Sydney) to William Wilberforce (?) Papers of Archbishop John Moore (as Filmed by the AJCP)/File 4'. 1794, 4 May 1794. Lambeth Palace Library. Image 3 http://nla.gov.au/nla.obj-1370817647.
[148] Collins. An Account of the English Colony in New South Wales. 253.
[149] Ibid, 257.
[150] Bladen, F.M., ed. 1892. *Historical Records of New South Wales (1793-1795)*. Vol. 2. Sydney: Government Printer. 1892-1901. http://nla.gov.au/nla.obj-359069774.

During the day, while he slept, Ann would have tended to their pigs, worked in the vegetable garden, and completed as many outdoor chores as possible. The greatest challenge would have been keeping baby Henry quiet.

The convicts generally had no respect for either Reverend Johnson or Reverend Marsden. When some convicts broke into the new church Johnson wrote "they found a bason (sic) upon the table where I baptize (sic) the children, & that they drank my health & the health of the new Parson."[151]

On the 17th of December Grose departed the colony, no doubt to secret cheers from Ann and her fellow convicts. Lieutenant Governor Paterson then took over until Governor Hunter arrived nine months later.

Governor Hunter, witnessing the damage caused by the military's rule, prioritised the reintroduction of civil government, and addressed the problems he identified. One issue was Sydney's contaminated water supply, which suffered from runoff laden with effluent from backyard pigsties. To rectify this, it was mandated that "any person found using a path from the house to the stream, or keeping hogs in the neighbourhood thereof, or opening a passage through the paling, will be removed, and the house pulled down."[152]

Another problem was alcohol. It was being smuggled in on ships and there were illegal stills making "a most noxious and unwholesome spirit, which not only serves to destroy the health of those who use it, but it also consumes a quantity of grain which would otherwise come to market."[153]

Governor Hunter ordered individuals like Samuel, responsible for maintaining order, to "be extremely vigilant in identifying and reporting any article or device used for the aforementioned purpose."[154]

He ordered:

> all officers, [etc. are to] use their utmost exertions ... to discover
> who those people are, who, self-licensed, have presumed to open
> public-houses for this abominable purpose. The Governor also
> informs those who may, after the publication of this Order, be daring
> enough to continue to act in opposition to its intention, that their
> house shall be pulled down a public nuisance, and such other steps
> will be taken for their farther punishment.[155]

He was attempting to reign in the military officers lucrative but damaging monopolisation of resources. Reverend Marsden wrote:

> there has been a great struggle between the Civil & Military Power.
> When Gov' Hunter took the Command he immediately put the
> Colony under Civil Government & directed the different Magistrates
> to do their Duty as formally (sic)- He saw & Comented (sic) the
> Dreadful state of Disorder, licentiousness, Idleness & dissipation
> into which the whole Colony was sunk- At the same time he had little
> prospect from the Officers in general of obtaining aid & Assistance

[151] 'Further Memoirs of Rev. Richard Johnson (44pp), Papers of Archbishop John Moore (as Filmed by the AJCP) [Microform] : [M677] 1793-1794./File 3'. 1794, 6 August 1794. Lambeth Palace Library. https://nla.gov.au/nla.obj-859140416.
[152] Bladen. Historical Records of New South Wales. Vol. 2. 327.
[153] Bladen. Historical Records of New South Wales. Vol. 3. 31.
[154] Ibid, 10.
[155] Ibid, 36.

*from them to enable him to reduce the Colony to any kind of Order
& Subordination.[156]*

In 1796, an abundant harvest of wheat and corn was achieved, thanks to the newly settled, fertile Hawkesbury region. It led to the colony being self-sufficient in grain. Reverend Marsden expressed his admiration for the Hawkesbury settlement, stating, "I think the settlement at the Hawkesbury is the most beautiful place I ever saw."[157]

During this time, imported goods such as tea, sugar, soap and clothing remained exorbitantly expensive, rendering them unaffordable for most officers, despite the "advantages from government."[158] Ann, could only dream of affording such luxuries.

1796 was the year Ann gave birth to their baby Maria[159] with her striking blue eyes.[160] Having two children may have strengthened the commitment between Ann and Samuel because soon after Maria's birth, a marriage was recorded on the 16th of April 1797 at St. Philip's Church between Samuel Holloway and Ann Jermie.[161] The wedding ceremony took place in a simple "temporary thatch'd (sic) house,"[162] built under the direction of Reverend Johnson four years earlier.

Three months later, Ann had another reason to celebrate as she completed her sentence and gained her freedom. Her feelings of joy and relief would have been tempered knowing that Samuel's life sentence showed no sign of ending. Being free Ann could apply for her certificate of freedom just like the men got. It proved that she was "at liberty to employ [her] time to [her] own advantage."[163]

Samuel provided the protection and security Ann and their children needed. The couple maintained a routine that seemed to work well, and Ann likely hoped for Samuel's eventual pardon.

Governor Hunter's strict stance on alcohol licensing began to soften. On the 19th of September 1798 seventeen men and women including Henry Kable, were permitted to hold licenses to retail "vinous and spiritous liquors"[164] in Sydney. The Licencing Court required that they enter into a recognisance and that they had a surety. Samuel was Henry Kable's surety, entering five pounds as the surety amount. Henry named his pub The Ramping House.

What quid pro quo did Henry offer Samuel in return? Had Henry been selling sly grog[165] and paying Samuel to look the other way? Henry was definitely

---

[156] Marsden, Samuel. 'S. Marsden (Parramatta) to [Unknown]'.
[157] Ibid.
[158] Ibid.
[159] Age 32 see '1828 New South Wales, Australia Census (Australian Copy) for Maria Bruce. (NRS 1272) 1828 Census Alphabetical Return. Surnames A-C. Image 167'. n.d. Ancestry. Accessed 1 May 2023. https://www.ancestry.com.au. and Age 20 see 'Registers of Baptisms, Burials and Marriages, Series NRS 12937, Reel 5002, Marriage Maria Howell V1815186 7'. 1815. Museums of History New South Wales - State Archives Collection.
[160] 'New South Wales, Australia, Gaol Description and Entrance Books, 1818-1930 for Maria Bruce. Entrance and Description Book. Sydney. Image 463'. n.d. Ancestry. Accessed 1 May 2023. https://www.ancestry.com.au.
[161] 'Registers of Baptisms, Burials and Marriages, Series NRS 12937, Reel 5002, Marriage Samuel Holloway and Ann Jermie V1797244 4'. 1797. Museums of History New South Wales - State Archives Collection. NOTE: With such a small population and no Samuel Holloway found in the records it seems highly probable this is Samuel Howell.
[162] Bladen. Historical Records of New South Wales. Vol. 3. 80.
[163] Ibid, 291.
[164] 'Samuel Howell- Bench of Magistrates Index 1788-1820, Item No: [SZ766] P90, COD 76, Reel 655'. 1798. Museums of History NSW - State Archives Collection.
[165] Implicating Henry Kable as encouraging an illegal still see 'Kable Henry: Bench of Magistrates Index 1788-1820 Item No: [SZ767] | Page No: 61 | COD: COD 77 | Reel No: 655'. 1799. Museums History New South Wales. NSW State Archives.

accumulating wealth at this point.[166][167]Or, was Samuel just doing a favour for a mate? Henry was the chief constable[168] in Sydney and would have worked with Samuel.

Children like Ann's boy Henry, who were aged over three, started getting some formal schooling in 1798. Reverend Johnson employed three men to teach them.[169] Being able to send Henry to school would have eased the demands on Ann, who had recently given birth to their third child, William.[170]

Most people were still avoiding church and spending their Sundays "in the indulgence of every abominable act of dissipation."[171] The Governor ordered the magistrates, to ensure that all public houses remained closed when church services were being conducted. He wanted everyone to attend but particularly the women. He said: "the women, who, to their disgrace, are far worse than the men be…ordered to attend divine service regularly, or they will expose themselves to punishment.*"[172]*

So, despite having a partner who slept during the day, three young children to care for, and a multitude of daily tasks involved in ensuring their well-being, Ann was also expected to attend church. As a free woman who was supposed to have autonomy of her decisions this smacked of hypocrisy.

It was no surprise when:

some wicked and disaffected person…took an opportunity of a windy and dark evening and set fire to the church. This building also serv'd (sic) during the week days as a school-house, in which from one hundred and fifty to two hundred children were educated.[173]

Then, on 4th of June 1800, Samuel's years of dedicated service on the night watch were recognised, and he was granted a conditional pardon. Governor Hunter said:

representations made to me in favour of Samuel Howell by the Judge Advocate, Provost Marshall and magistrates in Sydney, of his diligence and strict attention to his duty as a Principal in the night watch for upwards of eight years and in conformity to the encouragement [I] have usually given for a rigid performance of such.[174]

Granting this pardon was one of the last things Hunter did before the incoming Philip Gidley King replaced him.

[166] 8 Jan 1794. 30 acre land grant see Watson, HRA Vol1.1, 472. 14 Mar 1794.

[167] 15½ acre land grant see Colonial Secretary's Papers 1788-1825. KABLE Henry, [9/2731], Pp.18, 48. 1794. Museums of History New South Wales - State Archives Collection. https://content.archives.nsw.gov.au/delivery/DeliveryManagerServlet?dps_pid=IE4136770.

[168] 25 May 1802 " Henry Kable, having misbehaved in the execution of his duty, as chief constable, at Sydney, is removed from that situation." see Bladen. *Historical Records of New South Wales*. Vol 2. 771.

[169] 'Rev. R. Johnson (Sydney) to Gilpin. Fonds. Gilpin Papers/ Series MS Eng. Misc. c. 389/File Ff.252-54. (as Filmed by the AJCP)'. 1798, 5 November 1798. Bodleian Library. https://nla.gov.au/nla.obj-2060088120.

[170] Ann was listed with three sons and two daughters in Marsden's female list. See Marsden, Samuel. 1806. 'Samuel Marsden Essays Concerning New South Wales. We know that there was Henry Howell (1794), Maria Howell (1797), Hannah Howell (1803) and Charles Thompson (1805). This means that another son existed. In 1820 there was a Memorial to the Governor from William Howell aged 22, born in the colony requesting a land grant. No other matching parents for William have been found and his birth fits in the six years between Maria and Hannah. See 'Colonial Secretary's Papers. HOWELL William [4/1824A], File No.376, p.405'. 1820. Museums of History New South Wales - State Archives Collection. https://content.archives.nsw.gov.au/delivery/DeliveryManagerServlet?dps_pid=IE4149237.

[171] Watson, Frederick, ed. 1914. *Historical Records of Australia (1797-1800)*. Vol. 2. 1. Sydney: The Library Committee of the Commonwealth Parliament. 357. https://nla.gov.au/nla.obj-739303274.

[172] Ibid.

[173] Bladen. Historical Records of New South Wales. Vol. 3. 505.

[174] 'Samuel Howell- Conditional Pardon [4/4430]; Reel 774 p 012'. 1800. Museums of History New South Wales - State Archives Collection.

The wealthy landholders and military continued opposing government reforms. The trade in spirits continued and the merchants trading in sandalwood and whale oil continued building their wealth.

Figure 13: View of the west side of Sydney Cove 1804[175]

In 1803, the first newspaper, *The Sydney Gazette and The New South Wales Advertiser*, was published, providing locals with valuable information once a week. It was also the year that Ann and Samuel welcomed their fourth child, who they named Hannah.[176]

Figure 14: The first issue of the Sydney Gazette dated 5th of March 1803[177]

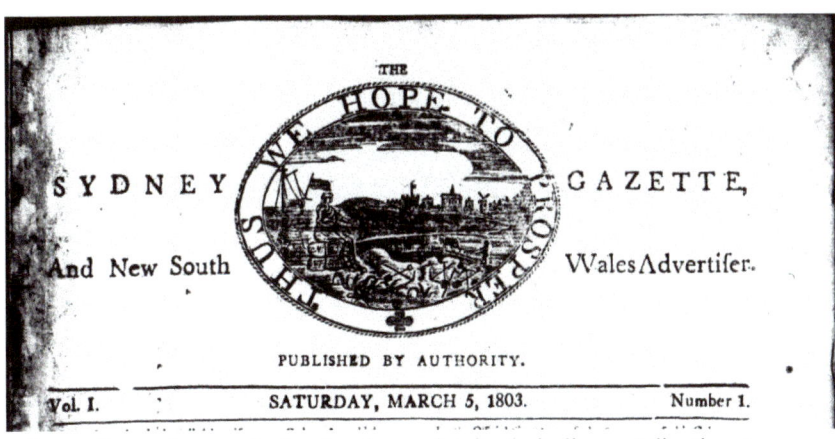

Samuel's pardon marked a turning point in their lives. Adjusting to normal working hours after years of night shifts disrupted the family's routines. Ann, who

---

[175] Eyre, J. 1804. *[View of Part of Sydney]*. National Library of Australia. https://nla.gov.au/nla.obj-135178991.
[176] Hannah aged 17 in 'Registers of Baptisms, Burials and Marriages, Series NRS 12937, Reel 5002, Marriage Thomas Dean and Hannah Howell V18202549 3A'. 1820. Museums of History New South Wales - State Archives Collection.
[177] *Sydney Gazette and New South Wales Advertiser*. 1803. '1803', 5 March 1803. 1. http://nla.gov.au/nla.news-page5653.

had grown accustomed to making her own choices during the day while Samuel slept, likely resented being told what to do, considering the societal expectation for wives to obey their husbands.

After four years had passed, Samuel's circumstances showed little sign of improvement, contrasting sharply with the rapid advancement in wealth and influence experienced by individuals like Henry Kable. Ann, no doubt feeling restricted, took the opportunity to leave Samuel when it presented itself.

She crossed paths with Bishop Thompson and the two Norwich ex-convicts no doubt had a lot of catching up to do. They had probably last seen each other when they left the Guildhall gaol cells and travelled to Portsmouth.[178] Meeting up again, sharing anecdotes about Norwich and memories of places they both grew up with would have been a comfort for two homesick people and they began a relationship.[179] Ann left Samuel and moved out to the Hawkesbury, to Bishop's place towards the end of 1804 early 1805. She took the children with her.[180]

Figure 15: Sydney Cove view to the west [181]

Samuel then found himself indebted to the ambitious Joseph Smallsalts. It appears that in October 1804, a promissory note in Samuel's name, was given to Smallsalts. The promissory note was a common method used in the cash strapped colony to allow the purchase of goods or services. This promissory note amounted

[178] *Norfolk Chronicle*. 1791. 'News', 5 February 1791. British Library Newspapers. https://link-gale-com.rp.nla.gov.au/apps/doc/GR3218762074/BNCN?u=nla&sid=bookmark-BNCN&xid=6af8fba4.
[179] Calculated from the conception of son Charles Thompson. He was buried the 21 Sep 1811 aged 6 years, i.e., conceived 1804.
[180] Marsden, Samuel. 1806. 'Samuel Marsden Essays Concerning New South Wales.
[181] Clark, John Heavside, John Eyre, and D.D. Mann. 1810. *New South Wales, View of Sydney from the East Side of the Cove*. National Library of Australia. https://nla.gov.au/nla.obj-3084876277.

to one pound, eighteen shillings, and three pence and was due to be paid in three months.[182]

Smallsalts, was living as a settler at Cornwallis on the Hawkesbury. He had somehow managed to secure a land grant of one hundred acres, even though he was a still serving his life sentence. The allocation was the same as that allowed for non-commissioned marine officers and far exceeded the thirty-acre allocation allowed for emancipated convicts.[183] He was benefitting "from many indulgences…received at various times from the Government."[184] As a convicted forger[185] he would have had a unique skillset which could have been exploited in the cash strapped colony. Could this be an explanation of why he was so favoured by the government, or did he bring other skills that had ingratiated him with the government?

Samuel put the following advertisement in the Sydney Gazette:

NOTICE.

SAMUEL HOWELL gives this public notice that no person shall credit his wife on his Account as he will not be responsible for any debt she may contract. Sydney, March 16, 1805.[186]

The advertisement not only shows that they he and Ann had separated but that Ann must have run up a debt in his name. It seems plausible that Ann, and not Samuel, contracted the debt with the Hawkesbury based, Joseph Smallsalts. There is no record of what the debt was for.

Joseph Smallsalts was inspired and influenced by Thomas Paine's *Rights of Man*. He held secret meetings in private houses.[187] Meetings that aimed to overthrow the monarchy's rule in the colony and form a republic just like America and France had done.

His plan was discovered a year later after meeting at old J. Pullen's house in the Brickfields. Two people who were at the meeting reported it to the authorities. His trial was reported in the newspaper:

S Y D N E Y

Joseph Smallsalts, a prisoner for life, was on Tuesday last brought before the Judge Advocate, charged with having uttered expressions of an inflammatory and seditious tendency, highly disrespectful of His Majesty's Government, and with intention to disturb the tranquillity (sic) of this Colony:— The facts alledged (sic) being clearly substantiated upon oath, the offender was ordered 100 lashes (which punishment was inflicted accordingly) and sent to public labour at the Coal mines at Newcastle. He was permitted to travel to Hawkesbury, in custody of a constable, to arrange his affairs

[182] 'Old Register [Electronic Resource]:One to Nine: The Registers of Assignment and Other Legal Instruments. Book 4, P6, Entry 1250. 1 Oct 1804.' 2008. DVD-ROM. Kingswood, NSW: State Records Authority of New South Wales. State Library of Victoria.

[183] 'Land Grants Guide, 1788-1856'. n.d. Museums of History NSW. Accessed 24 October 2023. https://mhnsw.au/guides/land-grants-guide-1788-1856/.

[184] *Sydney Gazette and New South Wales Advertiser*. 1806. 'SYDNEY.', 30 March 1806. 2. http://nla.gov.au/nla.news-article627066.

[185] *Northampton Mercury*. 1794. 'Wednesday and Thursday's Posts', 5 April 1794, Vol. 5, Issue 4 edition. British Library Newspapers. https://link-gale-com.rp.nla.gov.au/apps/doc/GR3218883688/BNCN?u=nla&sid=bookmark-BNCN&xid=3ed2e225.

[186] Sydney Gazette and New South Wales Advertiser. 1805. 'Classified Advertising', 24 March 1805.1. http://nla.gov.au/nla.news-article626697.

[187] *Sydney Gazette and New South Wales Advertiser*. 1806. 'Bench of Magistrates.', 30 March 1806. National Library of Australia. 3. http://nla.gov.aSu/nla.news-article627065.

*preparatory to his being embarked for Newcastle, with a label on his
back, on which Thomas Paine was decyphered (sic) in large
characters, the culprit having declared that "he would be worse than
Tom Paine if thwarted." [188]*

Ann's dealings with Smallsalts throw up intriguing questions. Was it just a one-off transaction for goods she may have needed when relocating to the Hawkesbury or was she more involved in the so-called seditious behaviour? Both she and Bishop grew up with the knowledge of their fellow Norfolk county-man, Thomas Paine's, ideas and words. It is easy to see how such a possibility would have inspired either of them.

[188] *Sydney Gazette and New South Wales Advertiser*. 1806. 'SYDNEY.', 30 March 1806. National Library of Australia. 2.
http://nla.gov.au/nla.news-article627066.

CHAPTER 5

BISHOP

On disembarking from the William and Ann in August 1791 Bishop and the other one hundred and eighty male convicts were described by Collins as very healthy, with only five requiring hospitalisation. Bishop would have been put to work as a labourer to help either produce crops or build infrastructure. The specifics of projects that he worked on and places he lived are not recorded, however by 1799 he was living at the Hawkesbury.

He had made numerous acquaintances by 1799, which implies he had been there for a while.[189]

When James Ruse and Charles Williams had arrived at the Hawkesbury in January 1794, they settled along a stretch of the river just east of present-day Windsor.[190] The success of their crops paved the way for the development of the area and soon there were more settlers, soldiers and plenty of convicts. It is possible that Bishop was sent to help in the cropping and development of the area at this early stage, however there are no records indicating his whereabouts. He had attained his freedom by 1797 and as a free man he had made a clear choice to be there in 1799.

The settlers had set up their ten and twenty acre lots on the lands of the of the Bediagal clan of the Dharug nation,[191] at "an important gathering place for ceremonies."[192]The land provided the Bediagal with all they needed, including vegetables such as donkey orchids, chocolate lilies, floating nardoo ferns, native cherries and native yams. The land was so productive that it was estimated to be supporting the most densely populated Aboriginal population on the continent, with over five hundred Bediagal people living between Sackville Reach and Richmond.[193]

[189] R. v. Powell [1799] NSWKR 7; [1799] NSWSupC 7. 1799. N.S.W. Court of Criminal Judicature.
[190] Collins. An Account of the English Colony in New South Wales. 246.
[191] In the area now known as Pitt Town Bottoms
[192] Ryan, Lyndall. 2013. 'Untangling Aboriginal Resistance and the Settler Punitive Expedition: The Hawkesbury River Frontier in New South Wales, 1794–1810'. Journal of Genocide Research 15 (2): 225. https://doi.org/10.1080/14623528.2013.789206.
[193] Ibid.

Figure 16: First Farms on the Hawkesbury 1794

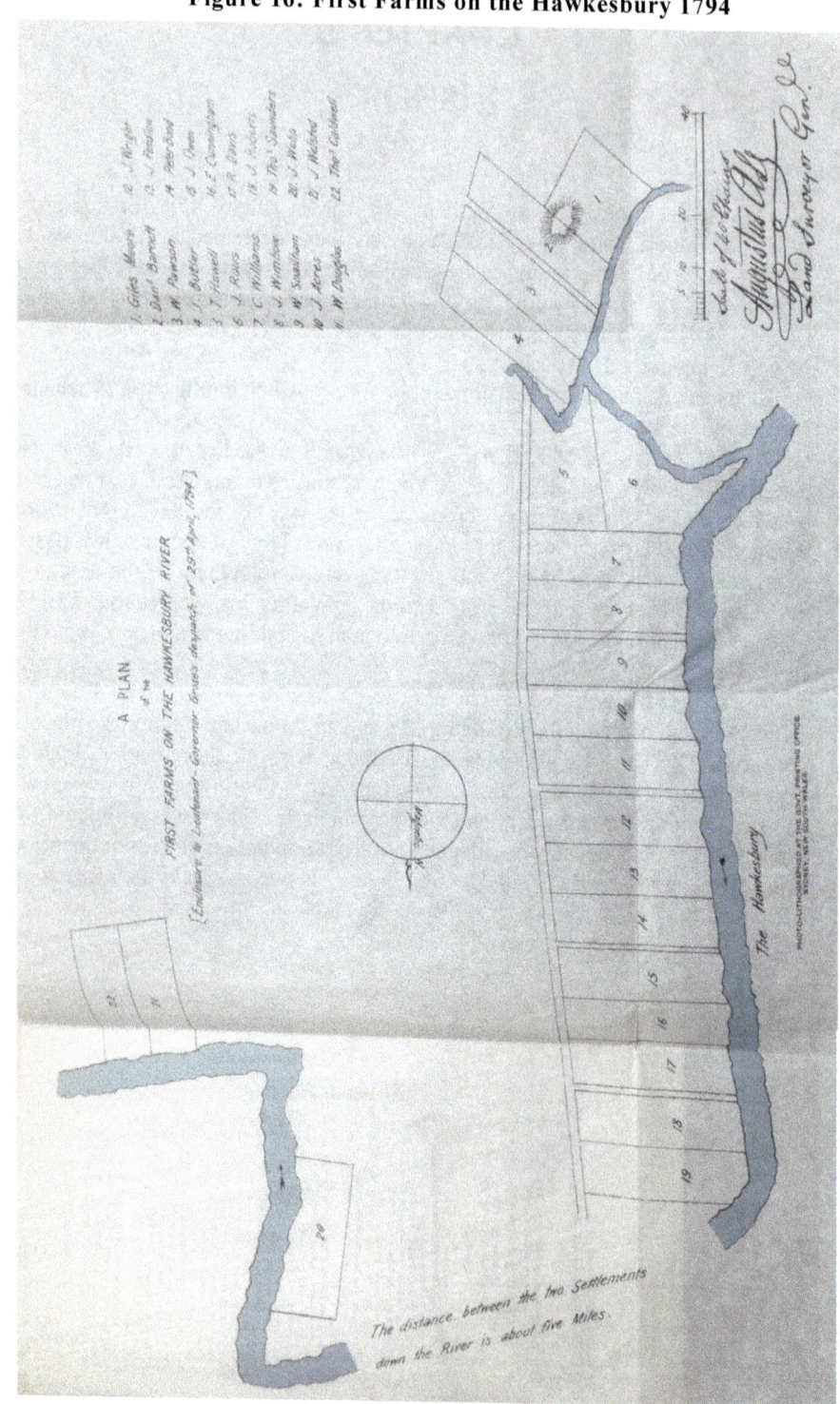

41

Their intimate knowledge of the land and mastery of living harmoniously in it, was too foreign a concept for the settlers. They paid "little attention...to the customs,"[194] and dismissed any idea they might learn from them. When Captain John Hunter ate some yams that were found growing next to the river he soon suffered "violent spasms, cramps in the bowels, and sickness at the stomach."[195] And acknowledged that the Bediagal people must have had "some method of preparing these roots, before they can eat them."[196]

There were exceptions, however. Glimpses of traditional knowledge were seen and occasionally documented. One man calling himself A. Woodsman wrote of his travels with local guides in the *Sydney Gazette*:

> On these excursions they never burthen themselves with any other luggage than a spear or two, and a short club, unless they have been fortunate enough to get possession of a tomahawk, which they very much prize...With an eye astonishingly acute they discern among the shrubbery as they pass the minutest trace of any object, they are in search, which by a sort of mechanical instinct they immediately dart upon and devour without any kind of cookery. A short white worm, weighing sometimes two ounces and perhaps more, they search after with avidity between the exterior and inner bark of the gum tree. At the distance of many paces, they discern a slight protuberance occasioned by its residence, though scarcely if at all discernible to me upon a near approach. A single stroke with the club they carry, in general drags the reptile from its confinement, and in an instant, it exists no more. Hence, we must still acknowledge that Nature has been bountiful to all her children; for although I could myself have submitted to death or famine rather than have partaken of a repast... The hive in its proper season, frequently affords to them a delicious solace ; the bees which they contain are small but numerous; and so regardless are their captors of any future benefit that might be derived from the labours of the swarm, that few, if any, escape the general massacre. The hives are formed in the hollow branches of trees; near to the butts of which some traces are perceived which betray the devoted hive, though not at all perceptible to me, even when pointed out...The hive brought within their reach, their next object is to secure the whole commonwealth...This honey I have very often tasted of, and its flavour exquisite; but I could not be persuaded to try the flavour of the bee itself, which my accidental companies appeared to be highly delighted with...
> In the various parts of trees that are decayed, prodigious nests of ants are frequently to be found; and after these they search with

---

[194] Corr, Barry. 2015. 'Pondering the Abyss: A Study of the Language of Settlement on the Hawkesbury Nepean Rivers'. *www.Nangarra.com.au*. 75. http://pandora.nla.gov.au/pan/144576/20160201-0000/www.nangarra.com.au/documents.html.
[195] Pages 103-106, Captain John Hunter, An Historical Journal of Events at Sydney and at Sea, Ed. J. Bach, Angus and Robertson, 1968, Originally published London 1793. Quoted in Corr.
[196] Ibid.

*unexampled assiduity. A glutinous substance, upon which I am
inclined to think the ant itself subsists, oozes from the wood, and is
sometimes hardened by exposure to the wind. Upon discovery of a
nest, they carefully lay it open, and with a little trouble mould the
gum, with perhaps whole millions of living subjects into one general
mass. While some are thus employed, others are rending from the
white gum tree the inner bark, which is remarkably fine; and having
procured a sufficient quantity they beat and rub it through their
hands until it is reduced to the softest state possible. This with the
nest is seated in the center (sic) of the group, who indiscriminately
separate small pieces from the coagulated lump, which carefully
wrapped in bark, they hold in their mouths until divested of every
particle of moisture.*[197]

Artist Joseph Lycett painted some hunting techniques (Figures 17-20).

Figure 17: Night Fishing[198]

[197] Sydney Gazette and New South Wales Advertiser. 1808. 'To the Printer of the Sydney Gazette.', 18 September 1808. 2. National Library of Australia. http://nla.gov.au/nla.news-article627586.
[198] Lycett, Joseph. 1817. *Aboriginal Australians Night Fishing by Fire Torches, New South Wales, ca. 1817.* Watercolour. National Library of Australia. https://nla.gov.au/nla.obj-138499378.

Figure 18: Using fire to hunt kangaroos [199]

Figure 19: Hunting Waterbirds in the Rushes[200]

[199] Lycett, Joseph. 1817. *Aborigines Using Fire to Hunt Kangaroos*. Watercolour. National Library of Australia. http://nla.gov.au/nla.obj-138501179.
[200] Lycett, Joseph. 1817. *Aborigines Hunting Waterbirds in the Rushes*. Watercolour. National Library of Australia. http://nla.gov.au/nla.obj-138501323.

Figure 20: Hunting Possums[201]

The Hawkesbury River is known as Dyarubbin to the Dharug people and it flows through both Dharug and Darkinjung Country.[202] When the settlers arrived in 1794 they were not the first Europeans to have entered the area. Since the early exploration in 1791 the area had been visited by hunters and by runaway convicts and was also the home of ex-convicts John Wilson and William Knight who were living with Aboriginal people.[203] The Dharug people had tolerated these incursions into their land. The explorers and hunters came and went without impacting the land too much and the weapons they bought were a big deterrent against attack. The Aboriginal people were also aware of the occupation of the lands at Sydney and Parramatta and the resultant conflicts, so when the settlers arrived the Bediagal people would have been horrified. They would have watched and evaluated the situation.

The settlers arrived unarmed[204] and the Bediagal people continued watching. The settlers set up on the yam grounds that were an important food source for the Bediagal and began planting their maize. They built huts to live in and pens for their animals.

In February the settlers were issued with firearms and then in April the maize crop ripened.

The Bediagal women whose role it was to harvest yams went to their yam grounds to harvest some maize. Their belief was that Country was providing for them and "they had a right to the maize."[205] The settlers saw it as theft and shot and killed one-man.[206]

Retribution was swift as a settler and his convict were killed in their hut.[207] The Hawkesbury settlers would have been aware that it was coming. They had seen revenge attacks practiced at Parramatta. In Aboriginal law "wrongs must be avenged…[and] family and friends of the guilty person could suffer punishment for their wrongdoing."[208] As Collins noted: "whatever the settlers at the river suffered was entirely brought on them by their own misconduct."[209]

After a few months there were seventy settlers at the Hawkesbury who had managed to clear some ground of the huge trees and planted wheat. The crop looked like the most promising one to date in the colony. "A very good road"[210] had been constructed from Sydney shortening the walk time from days, to just over eight hours, however, most supplies and people arrived via the river, using the colonial vessel *Francis.*

In October 1794, a report from the Hawkesbury confirmed that the settlers were committing atrocities against Aboriginal people. In what was a truly horrendous account Collins wrote that Robert Forrester, Michael Doyle and Roger Twyfield[211] seized a boy and "after tying him hand and foot, had dragged him several times

---

[202] 'Story Map'. 2020. Dyarubbin: Mapping Aboriginal History, Culture and Stories of the Hawkesbury River, New South Wales. 2020. https://portal.spatial.nsw.gov.au/portal/apps/MapSeries/index.html?appid=82ae77e1d24140e48a1bc06f70f74269.
[203] Karskens. People of the River. 122.
[204] Bladen. Historical Records of New South Wales. Vol. 2. 126.
[205] Karskens. People of the River. 132.
[206] Ibid, 133.
[207] Collins. An Account of the English Colony in New South Wales. 275.
[208] Karskens. People of the River. 132.
[209] Collins. An Account of the English Colony in New South Wales. 275-6.
[210] Bladen. Historical Records of New South Wales. Vol. 2. 254.
[211] Karskens. People of the River. 133.

through a fire, until his back was dreadfully burnt, and in that state had thrown him into the river, where they shot at killed him."*212*

Development continued with the establishment of a small government store to supply the inhabitants.[213] A mill was shipped on the *Francis* to process the grain into flour and a small number of guards were also sent to protect the store[214] and prevent attacks on the Aboriginal people.[215] It didn't work.

The Aboriginal people with no firearms, resorted to guerrilla warfare tactics. They attacked isolated settlers, burned crops and huts, killed livestock, and raided farms for provisions.[216] After eighteen months, the number of colonists on the banks of the Hawkesbury had reached approximately four hundred. They occupied a thirty-mile stretch on both sides of the river. The conflict continued to escalate. "Five people were killed and several wounded."[217] In response, a detachment of two subalterns and sixty privates from the New South Wales Corps was sent to defend the settlers. Unfortunately for the Bediagal people, they were going with a vested interest. As new landowners themselves they wanted the land cleared of Aboriginal people.[218]

Figure 21: A Hawkesbury farm looking down the river c1795[219]

[212] Collins. An Account of the English Colony in New South Wales. 277.
[213] Located in present day Windsor.
[214] Bladen. Historical Records of New South Wales. Vol. 2. 286-287.
[215] Collins. An Account of the English Colony in New South Wales. 282.
[216] Ryan. 'Untangling Aboriginal Resistance and the Settler Punitive Expedition: 219–32.
[217] Bladen. Historical Records of New South Wales. Vol. 2. 307-308.
[218] Corr. 'Pondering the Abyss'. 47.
[219] Wilson, Lowry. 1798. *Saunderson's Farm Looking down the River*. Engraving. National Library of Australia. https://nla.gov.au/nla.obj-135682235.

The night following the military's arrival, a group of Aboriginal people came onto one of the new farms. The military pursued them and killed seven or eight and captured one man and four women. They were held captive to be "made to understand that… we cannot suffer our people to be inhumanly butchered, and their labour rendered useless by their depredations, with impunity."[220]

September 1795 saw a flood height of twenty-five feet above the river's usual level, which caused the inundation of several settler's properties. "The rise of the river was so rapid that one settler was drowned."[221]

Then the summer of 1796-1797 saw drought and bushfires wreaking havoc. The strong winds and dry conditions caused "conflagrations of astonishing extent."[222] Properties, livestock and crops were lost leaving some people destitute.

The Aboriginal people on the Hawkesbury both fought and mingled with the white men. Decisions about who to fight were arguably "personal in nature"[223] and aimed at those settlers who were easy targets because of their isolation from the main settlements.

Governor Hunter in an attempt to prevent conflict between the settlers and the Aboriginal peoples ordered that:

> *for the general security of the farmers and their families, as well as*
> *for the preservation of their crops, that they should upon all*
> *occasions of alarm mutually afford assistance to each other by*
> *assembling without a moment delay whenever any numerous body of*
> *the natives are known to be lurking about the farms… The Governor*
> *Takes this opportunity of strictly forbidding the settlers from giving*
> *any encouragement to the natives to lurk about their farms.*[224]

In March 1799, Aboriginal intelligence about an approaching flood was ignored by the settlers, to their detriment. Many people lost houses, livestock, and belongings, and one person lost their life. The settlers were struggling, and no support was available from the fledgling government. They were on their own.

In about August 1799 an Aboriginal woman and child crossed paths with Private Cooper. He killed them and it set off a new wave of hostilities.

The commander of the military, Lieutenant Hobby heard that "it was the intention of the natives to come down in numbers from the Blue Mountains to the Hawkesbury and to murder some of the white people and particularly some of the soldiers."[225]

Joseph Smallsalts was travelling back from Parramatta to his farm on the Hawkesbury when he was attacked. He reported to Hobby that if he hadn't been armed with a musket and pistol, he would not have escaped. Spears were thrown at him, but he managed to get away.[226]

The next day, a report came from Andrew Thompson, a constable at the Hawkesbury, stating that Serjeant Goodall, a Marine settler, had been gravely injured in an attack by the Aboriginal people on his property and wasn't expected

---

[220] Bladen. Historical Records of New South Wales. Vol. 2. 307-308
[221] Ibid. 320
[222] Watson. Historical Records of Australia. Vol. 2. 1. 19-20.
[223] Corr. 'Pondering the Abyss'. 1.
[224] Bladen. Historical Records of New South Wales. Vol. 3. 25-26
[225] R. v. Powell [1799].
[226] Ibid.

to survive. Hobby also got a report of a killing of a settler on the race ground. After consulting the governor, he got a vague instruction to "act discretionally."[227]

News of the attacks spread to the general population and when William Bladely met up with Dharug man, Major White, he asked him: "why the natives were angry with the white men. Major White replied they were angry with the white men, particularly the soldiers."[228]

Another settler named Hodgkinson recruited three Dharug guides named Little George, Little Jemmy and another, possibly Charley to guide him and John Wimbow on a pheasant hunting trip.

John Wimbow was also known to Samuel Howell. The two of them had been sentenced on the same day at Winchester and were shipped out together on the *Scarborough (2)*.[229] There is no evidence they stayed in contact. Wimbow was one of the original settlers at the Hawkesbury and was Charles Williams' neighbour.[230] He had also been the man who had tracked, shot and killed Australia's first bushranger, John Black Caeser, for the reward of five gallons of spirits in 1796.[231]

Wimbow was reported to have been living with the daughter of Aboriginal man Terribandy, an offence that warranted Aboriginal retributive justice.[232] As he and Hodgkinson prepared to leave, the guides absconded "probably because of the presence of Wimbow…it is likely that the three guides left to tell Terribandy."[233]Hodgkinson and Wimbow set off in the direction of the Grose River, alone. Why they chose to travel so far to go hunting when ample locations existed much closer isn't known. After travelling all day, they came to "the second ridge of the Mountains"[234] where they met up with Terribandy, Major White and another. Tensions must have been high. Wimbow had been in the area for five years and must have known he had wronged Terribandy. All were armed. We only have hearsay accounts from the settlers as to what happened. They said that:

> They passed part of the next day together and toward the evening made a fire and eat, after which the said Hodgskinson (sic) and Wimbolt (sic) laid them down under the covering of blankets. That the said three other natives afterwards secured their two muskets and put said Hodgskinson (sic) and Wimbolt to death with their waddys. [235]

The statement doesn't ring true to the facts and appears to have been designed to portray Wimbow and Hodgkinson as being lured into a sense of security before being set upon two nights after meeting up with Terribandy. In all likelihood they would have been ambushed straight away. They definitely would not have slept and left their guns unattended knowing Terribandy was seeking justice.

[227] Ibid.
[228] Corr. 'Pondering the Abyss'. 28.
[229] Wimbow was sentenced at Winchester on the same day as Samuel Howell and arrived on the same ship. See 'Convict Indents (Digitised) Index 1788-1801. HOWELL Samuel and WIMBOW John, Ship Scarborough (2), Place of Trial: Winchester, County Hants'. 1789. Museums of History New South Wales - State Archives Collection. https://content.archives.nsw.gov.au/delivery/DeliveryManagerServlet?dps_pid=IE378703.
[230] See Figure 16.
[231] Cunneen, Chris, and Mollie Gillen. 2005. 'John Black Caesar (c. 1763–1796)'. In *Australian Dictionary of Biography*. Canberra: National Centre of Biography, Australian National University. https://adb.anu.edu.au/biography/caesar-john-black-12829.
[232] Karskens. People of the River. 140.
[233] Corr. 'Pondering the Abyss'. 26.
[234] *Sydney Gazette and New South Wales Advertiser*. 1804. 'SYDNEY.', 15 July 1804. 2. http://nla.gov.au/nla.news-article626311.
[235] R. v. Powell [1799]

The bodies were stripped of all their belongings and left to rot.

After a week or so Hodgkinson's heavily pregnant wife, Sarah began to worry when he didn't return. She went into labour and gave birth to the couple's third baby. Her worries were worsened when William Fuller saw a blanket, he had lent Wimbow being worn by an Aboriginal woman.

After a couple more weeks Lieutenant Hobby decided to send out a search party. He told the soldiers: "that if they fell in with any natives on the road either going or returning to fire in upon them."[236] Civilians who went on the search were under the same instruction. Amongst those who found the bodies were Fuller, Jonas Archer, Simon Freebody, Edward Powell and William Metcalfe. The horrific sight of the decomposing, naked, speared "and otherwise mangled"[237]bodies stayed with the men and fuelled their bitter attitude to the Aboriginal people.

Figure 22: Junction of the Hawkesbury and Grose Rivers, 1809. [238]

A couple of weeks later Jonas Archer found out from Yellowgowy that the men who killed Hodgkinson and Wimbow were Major White and Terribandy. He also learned that Major White had Hodgkinson's gun. The following day he told sixteen-year-old Little Jemmy to go and bring the gun in and he let Sarah Hodgkinson know what was happening. What incentive the boy had is unknown.

As the sun was setting on the 18th of September 1799 James Metcalfe was at work on Robert Forrester's farm when Jemmy approached bringing Hodgkinson's gun. He was accompanied by several men and boys including Major Worgan and twelve-year-old Little George. Each was carrying a spear, woomera and wadi. Metcalfe, the memories of the mutilated bodies fresh in his mind, received the gun

---

[236] R. v. Powell [1799]
[237] Ibid
[238] Evans, George William. 1809. *Collection 03: View of Part of Hawkesbury River at 1st Fall and Connection with Grose River N.S. Wales.* Watercolour. State Library of New South Wales. https://collection.sl.nsw.gov.au/record/YRlZvN2n.

and claimed that they said: "in a broken tongue"[239] that they were with Hodgkinson and Wimbow the night before the murder. He asked them into the house, but only three of the boys went in. Little Jemmy, Little George and one other. Forrester's wife, Isabella Ramsay and her children were inside. A neighbour John Pearson was also likely there.[240]

Metcalfe asked again about the murders. The boys replied: "not angry with any more white men, but very bad soldier, very bad them."[241] He then left, taking the gun to Sarah Hodgkinson. Metcalfe described the boys to her and she confirmed that they were the boys who were supposed to go as guides with Hodgkinson. Metcalfe continued on to neighbouring farms telling them "he had been alarmed by three natives on Forrester's farm."[242] Thanks to the Governor's order of 1796 requiring the farmers to assist each other whenever they were alarmed by the Aboriginal people, the neighbours had no choice but to drop everything they were doing and go and assist.

Simon Freebody, a landowner, was the first to arrive at the house. He decided to get Edward Powell, a constable. Powell spoke to Sarah Hodgkinson, the grieving widow who was filled with vengeance. She requested that he kill the boys.

Powell and Freebody entered Isabella Ramsay's house. Powell had premeditated his actions and said: "you have killed a good fellow and you shall not live long."[243] The boys "seemed much alarmed"[244] and tried to flee. Metcalfe arrived with some neighbours including William Butler, Thomas Sanburn, William Timms and Bishop Thompson. Powell interrogated the boys about Hodgkinson and Wimbow and terrified they fought to escape again. "Powell then seized the biggest of the three, and in taking him by the arm a tomahawk dropt (sic) from the sleeve of his coate (sic)."[245]

Butler, arrived armed with a bright cutlass and said: "what sentence shall we pass on these blackfellows. I will pass sentence myself. They shall be hanged."[246]

Powell said: "they should be killed for they have killed a worthy good fellow and it will be a pity to see them go away alive."[247]

Others, possibly Sanburn, Pearson and Bishop[248] disagreed. One said: "we will not kill them, we will carry them out as the means of finding the natives who killed Hodgskinson (sic)."[249]

---

[239] Ibid
[240] He stated in R v Powell that "he was accustomed to sleep and to keep the woman company." Metcalfe's statement inferring that he left the Aboriginal boys alone with Isabella Ramsay and her children doesn't add up. If they were armed and everyone was so scared, then he would not leave her alone with them. It seems possible they were having an affair and endeavouring to cover it up.
[241] R. v. Powell [1799]
[242] Ibid.
[243] Ibid.
[244] Ibid.
[245] Ibid.
[246] Ibid.
[247] Ibid.
[248] Mary Archer was the whistleblower on the killings and is regarded as "a person of principle" with "moral courage". See Corr. She reported that she heard (from Pearson) that "Sanburn, Thompson and Pearson had nothing to do with the murder." See R v Powell. Hearsay information.
[249] R. v. Powell [1799]

Figure 23: Property locations relating to the R. v Powell[250]

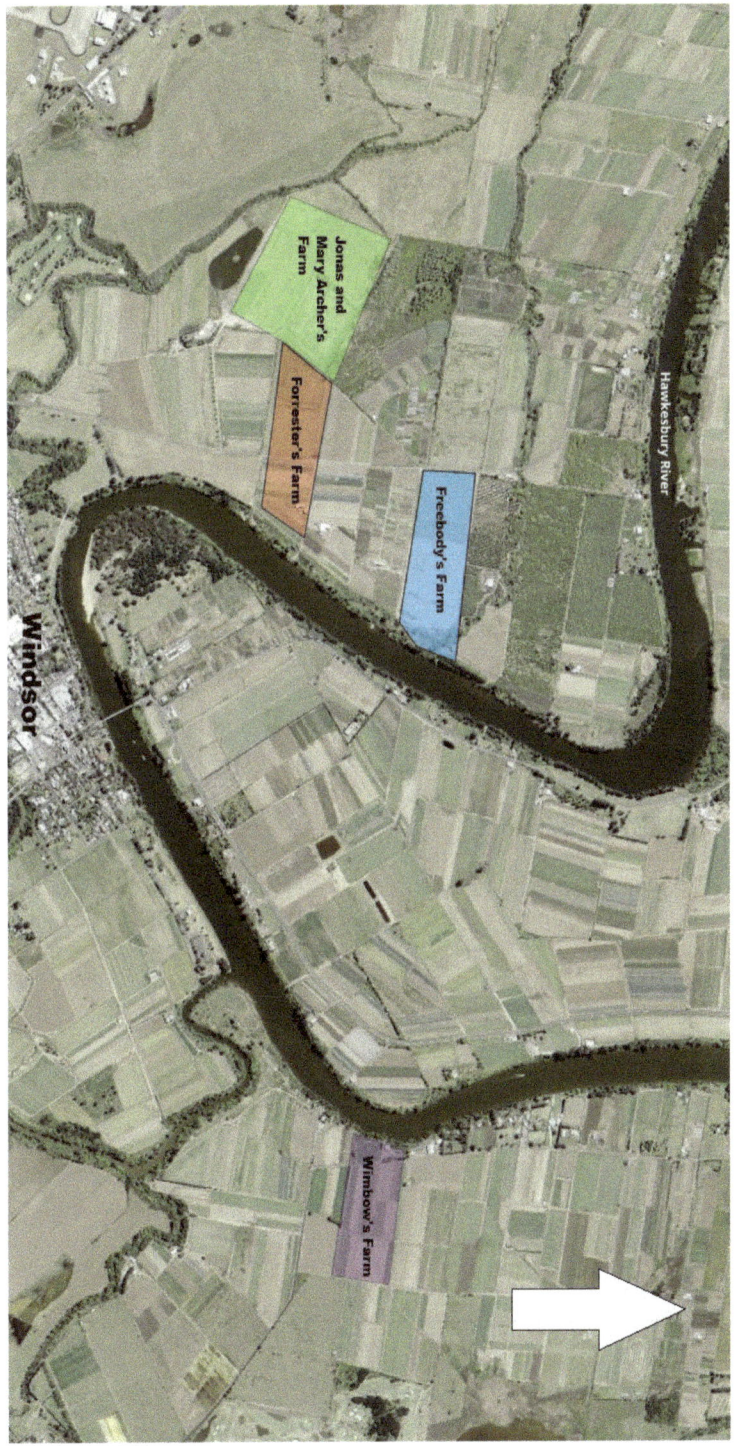

They asked the boys if any other Aboriginal people were in the area and they "answered there was another called Major Worgan out upon the ground."[251] Sanburn, and Bishop, went to find him.

With Sanburn and Bishop out of the picture Powell met no more opposition and organised for rope to be brought and for the boys' hands to be bound. At 10pm they were marched out of the house and ropes placed around their necks. Butler was holding the rope round the neck of one boy. The boy managed to make a dash for it. Powell shot at him and missed. Powell later claimed in his defence that he didn't have his gun as Bishop had taken it.[252]

The boy escaped. Freebody killed Little George by thrusting a cutlass into his right loin and through his heart. Little Jemmy was held by Timms while Metcalfe shot him in the chest. After they buried the bodies Freebody and Timms accompanied Sarah Hodgkinson back to her home.

The next day Mary Archer heard what had happened and went to the chief constable, Thomas Rickerby, to report the murders. He investigated and managed to get Sanburn to turn King's evidence. Sanburn swore to the truth of his evidence before the committing magistrate. This evidence is not recorded but considering that Powell, Timms, Metcalfe, Butler and Freebody were charged it seems probable that they were committed to stand trial based on his statement. A statement he refused to swear to in court.

Whether Bishop was questioned or not, is not recorded. The authorities may have concluded that he provided no additional information to Sanburn or he may not have been questioned at all. Thomas Rickerby appeared to conduct a thorough investigation so the logical conclusion is that Bishop probably was questioned but could not provide any additional information.

Why was he there and why didn't he speak up? As an ex-convict labourer, he had to tread a very thin line in this outpost. Required to obey the law and expected to obey his employer, he was open to exploitation. It has been suggested that "Single male convicts were at particular risk of an unrecorded paddock burial."[253]Bishop having earned his freedom would not have wanted to risk it by disobeying any authority figure or powerful landowner. He was at Powell's house with Sanburn, Metcalf, and possibly Timms the day after the murder. Were he and Sanburn being pressured to keep quiet by Metcalfe and Timms? Powell as a constable with a violent streak wasn't someone he would want to cross.

A month after the murder of the boys the trial started. Powell, Metcalf, Freebody, Timms and Butler were found guilty by a jury of military officers with limited legal knowledge. The court "refused to sentence them to death for murder without express instructions from His Majesty's Ministers at home."[254] So they got to return to the Hawkesbury to wait for an answer from England. Governor Hunter

---

[250] Map created by Lisa Apfel using Q-GIS version 5.15.3 and the NSW Land Registry Services Historical Lands Record Viewer Maps for County Cumberland Parishes of Pitt Town and St Matthew.
[251] Ibid.
[252] Powell stated in R v Powell that 'Bishop Thompson has my piece, and he is gone down to the ground'.
[253] Corr. 'Pondering the Abyss'. 2.
[254] Ibid. 99

disagreed with the decision but did not want to set a precedent by interfering with the judiciary. He was aware that there was conflict on both sides. The whites were:

> *wantonly destroying the natives. Much of that hostile disposition which has occasionally appear'd in those people has been but too often provoked by the treatment which many of them have received from the white inhabitants [and] the mischiefs which [the Aboriginal people] can do to us renders it highly essential to our own comfort and security that we shou'd live on amicable terms with them.* [255]

In 1802, Governor King received word from England that the men were to be pardoned. He was told to make "clearly understood that on future occasions, any instance of injustice or wanton cruelty towards the natives will be punished with the utmost severity of the law."[256] "How he proposed to do this while letting confessed killers go free is patently unclear."[257]

William Balmain, the Principal Surgeon of the colony and a magistrate, wrote in May that having officers acting as jurors was no longer satisfactory. They did not have the requisite legal knowledge to determine the increasingly complex cases. They often had to refer cases to English legal experts which meant "justice is left to sleep."[258] It caused the people to have no respect for the courts.

The growing settlement forced the Dharug people into more remote areas and the remote farms came under attack. By late 1809, the Dharug population was decimated by eighty percent through disease and violence. They "met Lieutenant Governor Paterson 'and were pardoned in exchange for promising to cease their attacks.'"[259]

---

[255] Watson. Historical Records of Australia. Vol. 2. 1. 402.

[256] Watson, Frederick, ed. 1914. *Historical Records of Australia (1801-1802)*. Vol. 3. 1. 367. https://nla.gov.au/nla.obj-739469879.

[257] Ford, Lisa. 2010. *Settler Sovereignty : Jurisdiction and Indigenous People in America and Australia, 1788-1836*. Cambridge, Mass. : Harvard University Press. http://archive.org/details/settlersovereign00lisa 99.

[258] Balmain, William. 1802. 'Series 23.03: Letter Received by Banks from William Balmain.', 24 May 1802. Sir Joseph Banks Papers. State Library of New South Wales. https://www.sl.nsw.gov.au/banks/section-06/series-23/23-03-letter-received-by-banks-from-william.

[259] Ryan. 'Untangling Aboriginal Resistance and the Settler Punitive Expedition: 228.

CHAPTER 6
LIFE AT THE HAWKESBURY

Bishop lived on a twenty acre block of land that he rented from Mr Palmer.[260] Some of the block was cleared but all around was a forest dominated by scribbly gums and native thorn bushes.[261] Ann had never experienced isolation like it. She must have had misgivings about her decision.

As they entered 1805, Ann and the children would have adjusted to their new home. Young Henry Howell was eleven and would have been able to help his stepfather with jobs on the farm. They were primarily cropping the land.[262] They would also have gone hunting, trapping and fishing to both supplement their diet and to protect their farm from predators. Frenchman Louis de Freycinet noted that the wild dogs were still in large numbers but the ruthless war that was being waged on them would soon see their annihilation. He also inferred that the peaceful kangaroos, were also being hunted to the same level so that people could: "[feed on their flesh and use their furs to make clothes or hats]."[263] Possums were also hunted for their long silky fur.

Eight-year-old Maria and seven-year-old William would have been given chores to do, to help Ann out whilst she raised them and two-year-old Hannah.

Ann fell pregnant again and nine months later safely delivered baby Charles Thompson.[264]

The wet weather that started in 1806 fell steadily for weeks, saturating the ground. It increased in intensity and by Friday the 21st of March Dyarubbin began showing the tell-tale signs of flooding. The water became muddy, speeding up and swelling. Some settlers started preparing to evacuate[265] but towards the afternoon the level appeared to drop, so many decided they would wait and monitor the situation.

Ann and Bishop, whose block was back from the river edge, likely stayed put. Their house was probably out of the flood zone (See Figure 24). They would have gone to bed and been woken by the sound of their neighbours firing guns in distress. One, resident said:

> *About half-past eleven I awoke and found the water almost up to the edge of our bed. Mr. Evans got the bed, with myself and children, up*

[260] 'New South Wales and Tasmania, Australia Convict Musters, 1806-1849, New South Wales, General Muster. For Bishop Thompson. Image 123'. 1806. Ancestry. 1806. https://www. ancestry.com.au.
[261] 'Scheyville National Park | Learn More'. 2023. NSW National Parks. 2023. https://www.nationalparks.nsw.gov.au/visit-a-park/parks/scheyville-national-park/learn-more.
[262] 'New South Wales, Australia, Colonial Secretary's Papers 1788-1856. Special Bundles 1794-1825. Bishop Thompson in Weekly Return at Hawkesbury 1809. Images 21133-21134'. n.d. Ancestry. Accessed 11 April 2023. https://www.ancestry.com.au.
[263] Freycinet, Louis Claude Desaulses de. 1824. Voyage Autour Du Monde, Entrepris Par Ordre Du Roi. Exécuté Sur Les Corvettes de S.M. l'Uranie et La Physicienne, Pendant Les Années 1817, 1818, 1819 et 1820. [Journey around the World, Undertaken by Order of the King. Executed on the Corvettes of H.M. Uranie and Physicienne, during the Years 1817, 1818, 1819 and 1820]. Vol. [t.3] (1824) [Text]. Paris: Chez Pillet aîné. 42. https://doi.org/10.5962/bhl.title.152367.
[264] Mutch. Reel 2125: Charles Thompson Burial 21 Sep 1811'.
[265] Bladen, F.M., ed. 1898. Historical Records of New South Wales (1806, 1807, 1808). Vol. 6. Sydney: Government Printer, 1892-1901. 824. https://nla.gov.au/nla.obj-375569940.

in the loft. Before daylight the water was in the loft, when we again
moved in the heavy rain to the ridge of the house, and through the
repeated fireing (sic) of guns a man...came over the river bank with
a boat and took us off the house...We had not left the house a quarter
of an hour before the whole was covered, and part taken away...We
was on the house three hours ; had we been left an hour longer we
must have been drown'd, or perished with cold. It must be
Providence alone that sent the man to our assistance...besides the
very great danger to himself and boat being dashed to pieces by logs
in crossing the river...we have lost everything; pigs, goats, wheat,
corn, and other valuables, are all gone.[266]

It was a "scene of horror [that] presented itself"[267]that Saturday morning. As the sun rose it became apparent that the river was still rising rapidly, and hundreds of people were clinging to the "tops of houses and rafts of straw."[268]

The rain continued through the day and people remained trapped as the night set in. Dogs who had swum to the safety of trees were heard howling.

On Sunday, the rain eased, and the waters started to subside. Nearly three hundred people had been saved but five had died. Some like Samuel Craft and his family had "miraculous escapes... [He had taken] refuge in his barn, which was washed down in a few seconds after they were rescued."[269]

The devastation to the area was extensive and "those in utter distress"[270] were quickly supplied with emergency provisions from the government store. The local magistrate, Thomas Arndell wrote to Governor King:

Most of the settlers, with their familys (sic), must be supplied from the store. I
have just now sent a boat to the relief, as informed, of nearly two hundred persons
that has been two or three days without anything, and some without clothing in the
woods...I beg leave to mention that if boats and men are properly employed much
may be saved.[271]

As the main cropping area for the colony the loss of wheat and maize was a great concern, and attempts were made to try and save the remaining wheat stacks from rotting by spreading them to dry.

Reverend Marsden who, in addition to being a magistrate was a landowner in the area. On hearing of the flood he decided to travel out there from Parramatta to "learn what I can, and see the state they are in."[272]This man of God acknowledged the great distress in "every part of the settlement "[273]but he was more concerned with saving the wheat. He said:

I had intended to have left the Hawkesbury last night; but the place was in such
confusion that I thought it would be better for me to remain to see what could be
done to save the little wheat and maize that the flood has left. Many of the men here

---

[266] Ibid. 827.
[267] *Sydney Gazette and New South Wales Advertiser*. 1806. 'HAWKESBURY, MARCH 27.', 30 March 1806. National Library of Australia. 2. http://nla.gov.au/nla.news-article627063.
[268] Bladen. Historical Records of New South Wales. Vol. 6. 827.
[269] *Sydney Gazette and New South Wales Advertiser*. 1806. 'SYDNEY.', 13 April 1806. 2. http://nla.gov.au/nla.news-article627080.
[270] Bladen. Historical Records of New South Wales. Vol. 6. 825.
[271] Ibid.
[272] Ibid.
[273] Ibid. 826.

have behaved very ill, and this morning one of them refused to assist, and told me he would not work. He said he was a free man and would not work. I immediately ordered him to be punished with as many lashes as Mr. Arndell thought he could bear...I found it necessary to appoint more constables, and to give each of them a warrant to confine all the men in their own district...to compell (sic) all, whether bond or free, to work. I have also directed them to strip the corn that is left standing, and to leave it to dry upon the stem, and to pull the maize that broke down, and to bring it up to the Green Hills for the women and children to shell.[274]

Governor King sanctioned Marsden's punishment of the "wretch"[275] and sent extra law enforcement to make sure his new orders were carried out.[276]

After reviewing the losses King reduced the rations.[277]

[274] Ibid.
[275] Ibid.828.
[276] Ibid. 829.
[277] Ibid. 830.

Figure 24: Inundation at the Hawkesbury 1806. Showing John Palmer's land[278]

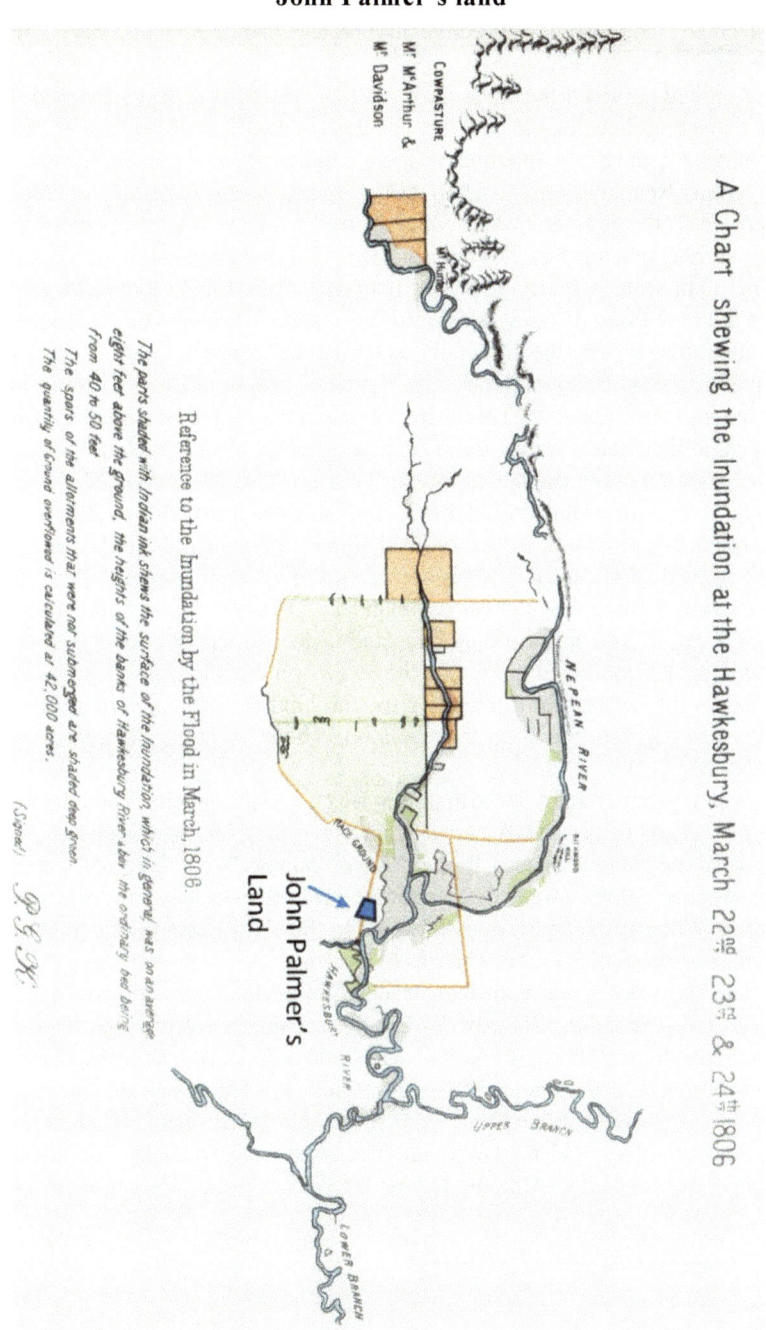

[278] King, Philip Gidley. 2015. 'Copy of a Chart Shewing the Inundation at the Hawkesbury March 22nd, 23rd, & 24th, 1806. Enclosure No. 2 / P.G.K.' [Sydney, N.S.W.][State Library of New South Wales]. State Library of New South Wales. https://collection.sl.nsw.gov.au/record/74VK7K6w3JoX.

Free men such as Bishop, whose livelihoods were lying in ruins, and their families destitute, were being whipped for refusing to save someone else's wheat. The greedy and divisive directive fuelled the hatred for authority. The people resisted.

Ann had survived but must have rued her decision to leave the city. She was back to struggling, again and the governor showed no compassion. Then four months later, the new Governor, William Bligh arrived. He set about redistributing the grain. Realising small settlers like Bishop were "destitute of seed,"[279] he appealed to the "humanity and benevolence"[280] of the wealthier landowners with their surplus to contribute "to the necessities [of those] who call for assistance."[281]

In addition to helping the poorer residents at the Hawkesbury like Bishop and Ann after the flood, Bligh was determined to make life more equitable for them. He set about dismantling the monopoly on trade that "the New South Wales Corps and a small handful of traders [had]… He tightened port regulations to control the flow of rum into the colony."[282] This change angered the people who had benefitted from it. People like Henry Kable and his partners James Underwood and Simeon Lord. They soon crossed paths with Bligh. In August, Bligh convened the Bench of Magistrates to trial Underwood, Lord and Kable because they had allegedly written a derogatory letter to the governor. It likely voiced opposition to the restrictions on their shipping business. They were sentenced to a month in gaol.[283]

Governor Bligh was a naval commander and his orders not only embittered the NSW Army Corps because they impacted them financially but because they were army men. He continued tightening the screws on the illicit spirit trade, saying, "he feels it is his duty to put a total stop to…prohibit the exchange of spirits or other liquors as payment for grain, animal food, labour, wearing apparel, or any other commodity."[284]

Wealthy settler John McArthur was Bligh's main opponent and also ex-army. On the 25th of January 1808 he was committed for trial for refusing to pay a fine. He faced the judge advocate, Richard Atkins and six NSW Corps officers and said that because Atkins owed him money he refused to be tried and the six officers agreed. When Bligh heard this, he wrote to the six officers the next day ordering them to report to him to face charges of treason.

The six officers met with their leader George Johnston who was acting under McArthur's direction. Johnson ordered McArthur's release and then illegally proclaimed himself the new colonial leader and ordered Bligh's arrest. That evening the self-proclaimed Lieutenant Governor Johnson led nearly the entire Corps to Government House where they arrested Bligh. "The specially created post of colonial secretary was bestowed on Macarthur who 'virtually administered' the colony until Lieutenant-Colonel Joseph Foveaux arrived,"[285]six months later.

[279] *Sydney Gazette and New South Wales Advertiser*. 1806. 'General Orders.', 24 August 1806. 1. http://nla.gov.au/nla.news-article627259.
[280] Ibid. 2.
[281] Ibid.
[282] 'From Terra Australis to Australia. The Main Players - Macarthur, Bligh and Johnston'. 2015. Text. State Library of NSW. 21 December 2015. https://www.sl.nsw.gov.au/stories/terra-australis-australia/main-players-macarthur-bligh-and-johnston.
[283] Bladen. Historical Records of New South Wales. Vol. 6. 278.
[284] Ibid, 253.
[285] Steven, Margaret. n.d. 'Macarthur, John (1767–1834)'. Australian Dictionary of Biography. Accessed 11 June 2022. https://adb.anu.edu.au/biography/macarthur-john-2390.

The overthrowing of the Government, an act that later became known as the Rum Rebellion was not supported by "many of the Hawkesbury settlers"[286]like Ann and Bishop. In part because Bligh had helped them recover after the flood, and also because they abhorred the wealthy, driven and self-absorbed[287] John Macarthur, who now had the power to keep looking after himself.

Ann gave birth in the mutinous year of 1808 to a daughter whom she named Sophia.[288]

Following Bligh's arrest the military rulers gave out many land grants and convict pardons "to Persons very undeserving of them."[289]Ann was amongst the many who were given a grant of land. Bishop being in the same situation may have benefitted from the military's allocations too but no record has been found.

The colony transition quickly through military leaders. Foveaux served just over five months being replaced by Lieutenant Governor Paterson for his second stint as colonial leader.

Norwich born Bishop, would have known little of farming when he had first arrived at the Hawkesbury, but he had slowly picked up the skills and knowledge and was rewarded with a harvest of his own wheat crop in April 1809. He managed to cut and transport three bushels to the government store[290] on the 22nd, then the following week he delivered one more bushel.[291] It was early in the harvesting season and prices were on the rise because the country was in drought which had caused the maize crops to fail. Wheat was in demand.[292]

Ann's relationship with Bishop had come to an end at about the time of the harvest which probably contributed to Bishop selling his wheat. The wheat used to make the family's bread was no longer needed.

Ann began a relationship with another Third Fleeter, James Hague. The circumstances of why she left Bishop for James remain lost to time. Women were known to be independent in this era, however Ann had baby Sophia and the five other children to provide for and would in all likelihood have moved straight in with James. What would make her want to leave Bishop and move in with James? Better opportunities, better security, or passion?

---

[286] Shaw, A. G. L. n.d. 'Bligh, William (1754–1817)'. Australian Dictionary of Biography. Accessed 11 June 2022. https://adb.anu.edu.au/biography/bligh-william-1797.
[287] "When an escaped convict was discovered on one of Macarthur's ships, the crew was detained on board ship as punishment. Macarthur reacted by disowning the ship, rather than supporting his crew," See 'From Terra Australis to Australia. The Main Players.
[288] Sophia was known as Sophia Bishop later in life, presumably choosing her father's given name. The reason behind her using this name may be an attempt to hide her origins as a child of convicts. Burial register states that she was a native of Scotland. There is no evidence that a Sophia Bishop travelled from Scotland to NSW before her marriage in 1827 to Alexander Dykes. He was from Scotland so is likely that the informant made the mistake or Sophia had lied to them. The only Sophia Bishop in the census and muster records was born in the colony.
Age 20 see '1828 New South Wales, Australia Census (Australian Copy) for Sophia Dykes. (NRS 1272) 1828 Alphabetical Return. Surnames C-L'. n.d. Ancestry. Accessed 5 May 2023. Image 157. https://www.ancestry.com.au.
Age 14. Sister to Mrs Bruce [Maria] see: 'New South Wales and Tasmania, Australia Convict Musters, 1806-1849 for Sophia Bishop 1822. New South Wales, General Muster, Image 46.' n.d. Ancestry. Accessed 5 May 2023. https://www.ancestry.com.au.
[289] Watson, Frederick, ed. 1916. Historical Records of Australia (January 1809 - June 1813). Vol. 7. 1. Sydney. 268. https://nla.gov.au/nla.obj-469139834.
[290] 'New South Wales, Australia, Colonial Secretary's Papers 1788-1856. Special Bundles 1794-1825. Bishop Thompson in Weekly Return at Hawkesbury 1809. Images 21133-21134'. n.d. Ancestry. Accessed 11 April 2023. https://www.ancestry.com.au.
[291] Ibid.
[292] Sydney Gazette and New South Wales Advertiser. 1809. 'SYDNEY.', 14 May 1809. 2. http://nla.gov.au/nla.news-article627744.

James Hague was emancipated and aged forty-three.[293] A carpenter by trade[294][295] he picked up work as a labourer[296] when it suited and had been in the Hawkesbury area for many years.[297] From this snapshot he would not appear to be offering any better opportunities than Bishop.

As a woman convention dictated that the children went with her, but again the records are silent. James a single man, had only ever needed a small place for himself, with just enough basic possessions to survive. One bed, one plate and one cup had been enough. Providing for Ann and her children would have been a challenge. She did, however, have her land and would have packed up their clothes and left.

On the 1st of June 1809 a flash flood hit the Hawkesbury.

> It was remarkable, that very little rain had fallen at Hawkesbury for several weeks previous, so that this calamity may rather be considered a phenomenon than as proceeding from any evident cause:—Many experienced Settlers attribute it to the bursting of a cloud upon the mountains, which overflowing the gulph occasioned the very sudden rise in the River. This disaster happening at a time when most of the Settlers had cropped their grounds, His Honor the LIEUTENANT GOVERNOR immediately ordered every assistance from the other Settlements, to facilitate the clearing and sowing the ground anew.[298]

Henry Kable ever the opportunist, followed Lieutenant Governor Paterson's instruction to help the settlers in sowing their ground. He offered to provide seed on credit for the local farmers.[299] Ann seeing an opportunity to get her farm planted approached him and agreed to his terms. He would give her the seed in exchange for payment when her crop was harvested.

Bishop was in financial stress after the flood and rather than approaching Henry Kable he went to one of the largest landholders in the district, Andrew Thompson, and made his deal. The man with the same name as his father, gave him some unspecified goods to the value of one pound and eight shillings and Bishop gave him a note of hand agreeing to pay it back. Then eleven days later on the 17th of June 1809 he was back making a similar deal for five pounds three shillings and sixpence worth of goods.[300] Andrew Thompson made similar deals with other locals, who were often wanting grain to use as seed for their next crops.

Exactly two months later:

[293] 'Registers of Baptisms, Burials and Marriages, Series NRS 12937, Reel 5011, Burial James Hauge V1849 971 34B'. 1849. Museums of History New South Wales - State Archives Collection.
[294] 'New South Wales, Australia, Settler and Convict Lists, 1787-1834, New South Wales. Male, for James Hague 1817. Image 219'. n.d. Ancestry Accessed 13 June 2023. https://www.ancestry.com.au.
[295] 'New South Wales, Australia, Convict Records, 1810-1891for James Hague. Musters, Muster of Prisoners in the Colony. For James Hague. Image 37'. n.d. Accessed 5 May 2023. https://www.ancestry.com.au.
[296] 'New South Wales, Census and Population Books, 1811-1825 for James Hague 1814. Population Muster, 1814. Image 8'. n.d. Ancestry. Accessed 12 April 2023. https://www.ancestry.com.au.
[297] 'New South Wales and Tasmania, Australia Convict Musters, 1806-1849, New South Wales, General Muster 1806. For James Hague. Image 72'. n.d. Ancestry. Accessed 5 May 2023. https://www.ancestry.com.au.
[298] *Sydney Gazette and New South Wales Advertiser*. 1809. 'FLOOD at HAWKESBURY.', 4 June 1809. 2. http://nla.gov.au/nla.news-article627755.
[299] Kable, Henry. 1809. 'Colonial Secretary's Papers, 1788-1825. Hawkesbury District. [SZ757], pp57b-58b. Reel No. 6001', 5 August 1809. https://search.records.nsw.gov.au/permalink/f/1ebnd1l/INDEX2399108.
[300] 'Court of Civil Jurisdiction. Andrew Thompson v Bishop Thompson, NRS 2659, Item 5/1103'. 1810. Museums of History NSW - State Archives Collection.

there was a flood here] the highest that was ever known by the white men it went over the tops of the houses and many poor creatures crying out for mercy, crying out for boats, firing of guns in distress; it was shocking to hear...Thomas Lacey, wife and family was carried away in their barn, standing on the man-made holes through the thatch and was taken out by men in boats and their lives happily saved...one was drowned and at the time the flood was at the height we all was in great fear we should be starved when the wheat stacks, barns and houses went. Many thousand bushels of Indian corn was washed away. We make bread of that instead of wheat. Most part of the wheat that was in the ground [was] killed by the flood.[301]

Kable who was experiencing financial pressures on many fronts and knowing he had already invested so much in the Hawkesbury settlers wrote to Lieutenant Governor Paterson four days after the flood. He proposed helping the settlers in need by further funding their next crops on the proviso that Paterson would agree to buy the future crop for the Government store at a guaranteed price. He stated that: "I am agreeable to risk [2 to £3000] to prevent the utter ruin of many industrious families who are now in a state of utter ruin and devastation from the calamity."[302] This was enough money to pay the wages of 20,000 skilled tradesman for a day.[303]

Paterson rejected the offer. Kable's offer, though couched in philanthropic terms, was a purely financial decision. He had invested so much and was now left with only one option and that was to enforce payment. Ann like many others having no crop to sell had to sign the deed of her farm over to him for "consideration money."[304]

The consideration money that Kable paid Ann is not recorded. If he had been as philanthropically minded as he had spruiked Ann would have had enough to put towards a roof over their heads and to replace any lost possessions, but she did not even have enough to keep her family together. Henry, Maria and William were sent off to Sydney and back to Samuel.

Ann also realised she was pregnant again.

Bishop's deal allowed him twelve months to repay his debts, however he still wasn't able to, and court proceedings were started. The provost Marshall served a writ on Bishop in August 1810 and told him that the court would hear the case in a month. Bishop did not to attend and was subsequently ordered to pay the full amount plus costs.[305] A month after the court case Andrew Thompson died and Bishop thought he might get out of paying it. By the 1st of February 1811 however the executors of Andrew Thompson's estate were in court seeking "to obtain

[301] Catchpole, Margaret. 1809. 'Margaret Catchpole Papers, 1801-1870. Letter to Mrs Cobbold from Richmond Hill.', 8 October 1809. Margaret Catchpole - Papers, 1801-1870. State Library of New South Wales. 16-17. https://collection.sl.nsw.gov.au/record/nQR2o3L1. Quote has had spelling errors corrected.
[302] Kable, Henry. 1809. 'Colonial Secretary's Papers, 1788-1825. Hawkesbury District. [SZ757], Pp57b-58b. Reel No. 6001', 5 August 1809. https://search.records.nsw.gov.au/permalink/f/1ebnd11/INDEX2399108.
[303] The National Archives. n.d. 'The National Archives - Currency Converter: 1270–2017'. Text. Currency Converter. The National Archives. Accessed 1 March 2024. https://www.nationalarchives.gov.uk/currency-converter/.
[304] 'Old Register [Electronic Resource]:One to Nine: The Registers of Assignment and Other Legal Instruments. Book 4, P3a, Entry 269. 14 Aug 1809'. 2008. DVD-ROM. Kingswood, NSW: State Records Authority of New South Wales. State Library of Victoria.
[305] 'Court of Civil Jurisdiction. Andrew Thompson v Bishop Thompson, NRS 2659, Item 5/1103'. 1810. Museums of History NSW - State Archives Collection.

execution under a judgement obtained in this court by the said Andrew in his lifetime against the said Bishop."[306]Again he didn't attend and again he was ordered to pay.

In 1809 when Ann sent her eldest children off to their father Samuel in Sydney, he had just become a father again, naming the baby James Howell.[307] The sudden arrival of his three older children would have been a burden, for his new partner Ann Martin and getting them employed would have been a high priority.

Girls like Maria were needed in domestic service and Henry at fifteen was soon apprenticed and training as a baker.[308] Even eleven-year-old William could get a placement as a boy doing odd jobs.

At three months of age, Samuel's infant son James, died. With nothing keeping them together Samuel and Ann Martin parted ways and Samuel looked for a new opportunity.

A year before, he had been employed on a voyage to Fiji collecting Sandalwood in the brig *Trial* under the command of Henry Kable Jnr.[309] Now looking for a new opportunity he heard that the new captain of the *Trial* was looking for "Twenty able Men to go on a pleasant Voyage to the Fejees (sic) and Society Islands."[310] he decided to go again.[311]

In the Hawkesbury, Ann gave birth to a daughter she named Dinah. Presumably in honour of her sister back in Norwich. The little girl's arrival coinciding with the new governor, Lachlan Macquarie's, arrival.

Macquarie was determined to rein in the self-serving military and their supporters. One of his first decisions was to cancel land grants and pardons issued by them, saying he would renew them "in my own name, in due time, when more fully acquainted with the Claims and Merits of the Individuals."[312]

Ann took the opportunity and applied for a new land grant. She had nothing to lose.

Bishop had not paid his debt and the provost Marshall was called in to clear the debt. The following notice appeared in the *Sydney Gazette:*

> *At Windsor, at Three in the Afternoon, THE Provost Marshal will proceed to Sell by Public Auction, a Stack of Wheat, the property of Bishop Thompson (unless the Execution thereon be previously superseded).[313]*

From this point Bishop's fortunes appear to have been on a downward trajectory. He approached Samuel Craft at Windsor, on the 6th of June and wrote him a promissory note for over forty-six pounds worth of goods.[314]This was

[306] 'Court of Civil Jurisdiction. H.C. Antill & T Moore Esqrs Exors v Bishop Thompson, NRS 2659-2, Item 5/1105'. 1811. Museums of History NSW - State Archives Collection.

[307] Mutch. 'Reel 2125: James Howell Baptism and Burial, 1809'.

[308] 'Registers of Baptisms, Burials and Marriages, Series NRS 12937, Reel 5002, Marriage Henry Howell V1815 151 7'. 1815. Museums of History New South Wales - State Archives Collection.

[309] *Sydney Gazette and New South Wales Advertiser*. 1808. 'Secretary's Office, December 17, 1808', 18 December 1808. National Library of Australia. http://nla.gov.au/nla.news-article627646.

[310] *Sydney Gazette and New South Wales Advertiser*. 1809. 'Classified Advertising', 5 November 1809. 1. http://nla.gov.au/nla.news-article627854.

[311] *Sydney Gazette and New South Wales Advertiser*. 1809. 'Classified Advertising', 24 December 1809. 2. http://nla.gov.au/nla.news-article627885.

[312] Ibid.

[313] *Sydney Gazette and New South Wales Advertiser*. 1811. 'Classified Advertising', 23 March 1811. 2. http://nla.gov.au/nla.news-article628214.

[314] 'Court of Civil Jurisdiction. Samuel Craft v Bishop Thompson, NRS 2659-2, Item 5/1107'. 1812. Museums of History NSW - State Archives Collection.

equivalent to a year's wages[315], which shows he had plans for some sort of major project. This was followed by another debt for four pounds on the 4th of September to Lawrence May.[316]

Ann's fortunes, however, were looking up. Her application for a land grant was confirmed on the 12th of June. She was getting fifty acres at Kurrajong,[317] "as soon as the acting surveyor can measure [it] out."[318]

Her world was then rocked, when her son Charles Thompson, at just six years old, was involved in a tragic accident. The details are lost to history except for a simple statement on his burial record saying "burned."[319] Bishop who was living at Freeman's Reach and Ann buried their boy on the 21st of September 1811. No doubt blame and anger would have been mixed with grief. The resilience Ann had needed, time and again throughout her many trials and tribulations would have been shattered. Knowing Charles's death was preventable would have been an almost unbearable thought. She had to go on though because she still had her three girls Hannah, Sophia and Dinah, relying on her.

For the illiterate people of the colony word of mouth was critical to learning about events that were happening. Ann would have regularly had conversations in town where she would have heard about the news of the day. Some news, like the crossing of the Blue Mountains[320] by white men had no real interest for her, but some news like the introduction of the colony's own official currency did.[321]

In April 1812 Bishop was served a writ to appear in court. Samuel Craft was wanting his payment. With such a large amount at stake Bishop made the trip to Sydney. Whether he thought he could mount some defence is not stated. The proceedings simply record that: "defendant [Bishop] personally appears in court and admits the same."[322] The judgement for Craft was for the forty-six pounds owed plus nearly two pounds in costs. Then in July Lawrence May also sought payment for the money he was owed. Bishop didn't appear this time and was ordered to pay the four pounds he owed plus over four pounds in costs.[323]

The next year Charles Beasley, a dealer in Windsor was willing to take a promissory note from Bishop. He sold Bishop some goods and delivered them to his home at Freeman's Reach. By April 1814 the all too familiar scenario was unfolding when Bishop was served a writ to attend court. He chose not to go. The court records indicate that he had managed to pay four pounds off the nine-pound debt but in the end, he was ordered to pay the remainder of the debt plus costs. Bishop did not pay the amount and the court issued a writ of fieri facias on the 9th of May.[324] This was an order directing the provost Marshall to seize and sell goods belonging to Bishop to cover the debt.

[315] The National Archives. n.d. 'The National Archives - Currency Converter.
[316] 'Court of Civil Jurisdiction. Lawrence May v Bishop Thompson, NRS 2659-2, Item 5/1108'. 1812. Museums of History NSW - State Archives Collection.
[317] 'New South Wales, Australia, Colonial Secretary's Papers, 1788-1856. For Ann Germay 12 Jun 1811- Special Bundles, 1794-1825. Image 1229'. n.d. Ancestry. Accessed 11 April 2023. https://www.ancestry.com.au.
[318] Ibid. Image 1227.
[319] Mutch. 'Reel 2125: Charles Thompson Burial 21 Sep 1811'.
[320] Sydney Gazette and New South Wales Advertiser. 1814. 'Classified Advertising', 12 February 1814. 1. http://nla.gov.au/nla.news-article628859.
[321] 'Holey Dollar'. undated. National Museum of Australia. undated. https://www.nma.gov.au/explore/collection/highlights/holey-dollar.
[322] 'Court of Civil Jurisdiction. Samuel Craft v Bishop Thompson.
[323] 'Court of Civil Jurisdiction. Lawrence May v Bishop Thompson.
[324] 'Court of Civil Jurisdiction. Charles Beasley v Bishop Thompson, NRS 2659-2, Item 5/1110'. 1814. Museums of History NSW - State Archives Collection.

Figure 25: The Green Hills [Windsor] 1809[325]

A muster of the population was undertaken in 1814. It was not comprehensive and missed many people including Bishop and Henry Kable. Ann, however, was recorded. She was at home and listed with only two children.[326] Presumably this would be her youngest two children, Sophia age six and Dinah aged four. The most likely whereabouts of eleven-year-old Hannah would have been with her father, Samuel in Sydney.[327] She was not recorded at his place in the census but that was not unusual as children were only recorded next to their mothers.[328] Ann also listed herself as Samuel's wife, which was technically true given that divorce was not an option. She however remained in Windsor while Samuel remained in Sydney. Ann's partner James stated that he was working as a labourer.[329]In Sydney the oldest children were standing on their own feet. Maria was single and supporting herself,[330]William had got himself an apprenticeship[331] training to be just like his father as a smith[332] and Henry was working as a baker.

After the Blue Mountains were crossed a road was quickly built and completed early in 1815. The same year that both Henry and Maria met and married their

[325] 'Series 01: Australian Paintings by J.W. Lewin, G.P. Harris, G.W. Evans and Others, 1796-1809: Volume 3. f.7 "The Green Hills..."' 1809. Mitchell Library, State Library of New South Wales. https://collection.sl.nsw.gov.au/record/YoldQAA9/groKMN3JaexNk.

[326] 'New South Wales, Census and Population Books, 1811-1825 for Ann Germaine 1814. Population Muster. Image 38.' n.d. Ancestry. Accessed 5 May 2023. https://www.ancestry.com.au.

[327] Author's deduction. Hannah being sent to Sydney is the most likely scenario for which of Ann's three youngest girls had left home in 1814. She was the eldest of the three. She was Samuel's daughter and her older siblings had already gone back to Sydney. Maria stayed close to Hannah as witness to her marriage and Maria also took in Sophia in 1822 as listed in the 1822 Muster.

[328] 'New South Wales, Census and Population Books, 1811-1825 for Saml Howell 1814. Population Muster. Image 88.' n.d. Ancestry. Accessed 9 May 2023. https://www.ancestry.com.au.

[329] 'New South Wales, Census and Population Books, 1811-1825 for James Hague. Population Muster, 1814. Image 8'. 1814. Ancestry. 1814. https://www. ancestry.com.au.

[330] 'New South Wales, Census and Population Books, 1811-1825 for Maria Howell 1814. Population Muster. Image 127.' n.d. Ancestry. Accessed 9 May 2023. https://www.ancestry.com.au.

[331] 'New South Wales, Census and Population Books, 1811-1825 for Will Howell 1814. Population Muster. Image 96'. n.d. Ancestry. Accessed 9 May 2023. https://www. ancestry.com.au.

[332] 'New South Wales, Census and Population Books, 1811-1825 for Will Howell. Population Muster, 1819. Image 100'. 1819. Ancestry. 1819. https://www. ancestry.com.au.

spouses. Henry married Mary Hill the daughter of the superintendent of the slaughterhouse, William Hill.[333][334][335] Maria was a witness to the ceremony. Then six months later Maria married William Bruce.[336] She asked her dad, Samuel to give her away and witness the ceremony.

In Windsor, James started listing himself as a landholder.[337] He and Ann were settled, and she could now see her struggles bearing fruit. Henry and Maria were doing well which would have been both a relief and a source of pride for her. Then Ann received the news that she was a grandmother. Nothing could have matched her joy except when Henry told her that he had named his daughter Ann.[338]

Maria had her first baby in the following year, 1817, a little boy named William, the same as his father.

Windsor kept expanding and Governor Macquarie made an official visit to lay the foundation stone to the new church that was called St Matthew's.

Figure 26: Foundation Stone of St Matthew's Church

As the number of Ann's descendants grew, she probably only got updates on their big life events. In 1818 she would have heard the happy news from Henry, that his second daughter Sarah[339] had been born and then the distressing news from Maria, that her baby William had died.[340] Samuel had become a new father again

[333] 'Registers of Baptisms, Burials and Marriages, Series NRS 12937, Reel 5002, Marriage Henry Howell V1815151 7'. 1815. Museums of History New South Wales - State Archives Collection.
[334] 'New South Wales, Australia, Colonial Secretary's Papers, 1788-1856 for William Hill 17 Sep 1817. Special Bundles, 1794-1825. Images 5448-5453.' n.d. Ancestry. Accessed 9 May 2023. https://www.ancestry.com.au.
[335] 'New South Wales, Australia, Land Grants, 1788-1963 for Mary Howell 1831. Registrar General, Deeds Registration Branch, Registers of Memorials, 1826-1831. Image 228.' n.d. Ancestry. Accessed 10 May 2023. https://www.ancestry.com.au.
[336] 'Registers of Baptisms, Burials and Marriages, Series NRS 12937, Reel 5002, Marriage Maria Howell V1815186 7'. 1815. Museums of History New South Wales - State Archives Collection.
[337] *Sydney Gazette and New South Wales Advertiser*. 1816. 'GOVERNMENT PUBLIC NOTICE.', 23 November 1816. National Library of Australia.1. http://nla.gov.au/nla.news-article2176911.
[338] Ann age 13 in '1828 New South Wales, Australia Census (Australian Copy) for Henry Howell. (NRS 1272)1828 Census: Alphabetical Return. Surnames C-L. Image 436'. n.d. Ancestry. Accessed 24 April 2023. https://www.ancestry.com.au.
[339] Mutch. 'Reel 2125: 1787-1814 from Abbott to Tillet. Sarah Howell Baptism, 1818'.
[340] 'Registers of Baptisms, Burials and Marriages, Series NRS 12937, Reel 5002, Burial William Bruce V1818 698 7'. 1818. Museums of History New South Wales - State Archives Collection.

at fifty three, managing to attract a much younger Irish convict named Bridget Cassidy. They named their baby Mary Howell.[341]

Samuel's new family responsibilities were the catalyst for him to apply for a land grant. He used some poetic licencing by saying he had "a large family."[342]True, but as most of his children were now grown, he only had Hannah and the new baby to support. Governor Macquarie approved his application granting him fifty acres.

Hannah at fifteen was at the age when many young girls started working. Her sister Maria was pregnant and, fearful of losing another baby, may have taken Hannah in to help her.[343] Maria had her new baby boy, Edward, in September 1819.[344]

Towards the end of the year a case was brought against Ann and James by William Baker, the publican of The Royal Oak at Windsor and local auctioneer. He was suing to recover £20 for goods he supplied to them.[345]Ann and James received a knock at their door in Windsor on the 30th of December. On opening it up they saw George Smith, the bailiff, who promptly handed them a summons to appear at the Governor's Court on the 24th of January 1820.

The court proceedings were not recorded, however the legal costs were listed and amounted to seven pounds and six pence, and the final judgement was noted as thirteen pounds, one shilling and two pence.[346] This was a significant amount for Ann and James and would have impacted on their lives. In England in 1820 it equated to almost three months wages for a skilled tradesman.[347]

On the 22nd of May 1820 Hannah was married to an ex-convict named Thomas Dean. Maria was right by Hannah's side at the ceremony and signed as a witness. Thomas was thirty-five, more than double her age. None of the parents (Ann, James or Samuel) were witnesses.[348] She moved into her new home in Eastern Creek shortly after.[349]

Maria, having lost her help, needed a replacement, so she appears to have approached Ann again. This time asking if twelve-year-old Sophia could be her domestic help. Ann agreed. A combination of factors was at play. In addition to the recent financial blow that Ann had taken, she understood the struggles that Maria was having being a new mother with no support and she also knew that Sophia had limited opportunities at Windsor. Maria's husband William, who was supportive of the idea, was in a good position to take her in.

The people of the colony who wanted to apply for 'indulgences' such as land grants, allocation of cattle, pardons or tickets-of-leave had to do so on specific days and in a specific manner. The governor had published a number of orders in the newspaper to inform the public of the process. In the case of land grants, applications had to be submitted on the first Monday in June. Back in 1818 there

---

[341] Mutch. 'Reel 2125. Mary Howell Baptism'.

[342] 'New South Wales, Australia, Colonial Secretary's Papers, 1788-1856 for Samuel Howell 10 Sep 1818. Special Bundles, 1794-1825. Image 1270'. n.d. Ancestry. Accessed 4 May 2023. https://www.ancestry.com.au.

[343] William Bruce was listed as employing Sophia in the 1822 Muster. This shows he was willing to house Maria's family.

[344] 'Registers of Baptisms, Burials and Marriages, Series NRS 12937, Reel 5002, Baptism Edward Bruce V1819 91 8'. 1819. Museums of History New South Wales - State Archives Collection.

[345] 'Governor's Court Case Papers 1815-1824-Ann Howell and James Hague. Case No 130, Series NRS 4563, Item No [4/7862] Index Number 76'. 1820. NSW State Archives.

[346] Ibid.

[347] The National Archives. n.d. 'The National Archives - Currency Converter.

[348] Lake Macquarie Family History Group. 2003. St Matthew's Church of England, Windsor, NSW.: Parish Registers, 1810-1856: 'A Complete Transcription'. 1st ed. Vol. 1. Teralba, N.S.W.: Lake Macquarie Family History Group. 130.

[349] Mutch. 'Reel 2127: 1815-1957 from Curtis to Jurd. James Dean Baptism and Burial, 1825 and 1826.'

were so many applications received and so little land available that the governor decided that no applications would be accepted in 1819.[350] As a consequence by the time the first Monday in June 1820 rolled around there were many people wanting to apply. Amongst them were Bishop Thompson, William Bruce, Henry Howell and William Howell. The four men followed the process of going to their local magistrate for vetting. The local magistrates and chaplains signed off on their applications which were then forwarded to the governor for approval. The governor decided how much land they were eligible for.

Bishop's application was submitted at Richmond and stated: "[he had] been free upwards of twenty three years, has a wife and three children and having ever since conducted himself with sobriety, honesty, and industry."[351] It was approved, and he was granted fifty acres.[352] His statement about having a family would have increased his chances of being successful. No records of him having a new family have been found, which is not conclusive that none existed, it is however highly unlikely. The three children were probably Hannah, Sophia and Dinah which was really stretching the truth since Hannah had just married, and Sophia had moved to Sydney. Magistrate William Cox and Chaplain John Cross had signed knowing that the governor had said:

> The Magistrates and Chaplains are requested to be very particular
> in giving their Signatures of Recommendations to Memorials for
> Lands, without being fully satisfied that the Applicants are deserving
> such Indulgencies, from Habits of Sobriety and Industry; and that it
> is their intention to settle and cultivate such lands.[353]

If both men were 'particular' and knew Bishop, then they too were complicit in stretching the truth.

Maria's husband William was successful in being approved for sixty acres as were her brothers Henry and William.[354] [355] [356]

As Ann heard about the land grants that her children had received, she would also have been told that Samuel and his young partner Bridget had had another son named Samuel.[357]

Twelve-year-old Sophia's move to Sydney would have filled her with excitement and a bit of trepidation. She embraced the change wholeheartedly and never looked back. By the time she was fourteen she had decided to distance herself from the shame of having convict parents and chose to use her father's name as her new surname. Now calling herself Sophia Bishop.[358]

[350] *Sydney Gazette and New South Wales Advertiser.* 1819. 'GOVERNMENT AND GENERAL ORDERS.', 22 May 1819. 1. http://nla.gov.au/nla.news-article2178714.
[351] 'New South Wales Colonial Secretary's Papers, 1788-1825 for Bishop THOMPSON. [4/1825B], File No.733, Pp.791-5.' 1820. Museums of History New South Wales - State Archives Collection.
[352] 'New South Wales Colonial Secretary; NRS-899 Memorials to the Governor, 1810-1826, Fiche 3032. Bishop Thompson to Governor Macquarie. Pp791-792'. 1820, 1820. Museums of History New South Wales - State Archives Collection.
[353] *Sydney Gazette and New South Wales Advertiser.* 1820. 'GOVERNMENT AND GENERAL ORDERS.', 20 May 1820. 1. http://nla.gov.au/nla.news-article2179480.
[354] 'New South Wales, Australia, Colonial Secretary's Papers, 1788-1856 for William Bruce 1820. Memorials to the Governor, 1810-1826. Images 1172-1179.' n.d. Ancestry. Accessed 14 May 2023. https://www.ancestry.com.au.
[355] 'New South Wales, Australia, Colonial Secretary's Papers, 1788-1856 for Henry Howell 1820. Memorials to the Governor, 1810-1826. Image 1690.' n.d. Ancestry. Accessed 15 May 2023. https://www.ancestry.com.au.
[356] 'New South Wales, Australia, Colonial Secretary's Papers, 1788-1856 for William Howell 1820. Memorials to the Governor, 1810-1826. Image 1696.' n.d. Ancestry. Accessed 15 May 2023. https://www.ancestry.com.au.
[357] Mutch. ' Reel 2125: Samuel Howell Baptism 1819'
[358] 'New South Wales and Tasmania, Australia Convict Musters, 1806-1849 for Sophia Bishop 1822. New South Wales, General Muster, Image 46.' n.d. Ancestry. Accessed 5 May 2023. https://www.ancestry.com.au.

By the time Ann turned fifty-two she would have been feeling the ravages of a hard life. Her youthful looks would have long faded, and she probably had greying hair, wrinkles and many teeth missing, thanks to little dental care. She was probably content to a degree receiving updates as each new grandchild arrived, although she undoubtedly would have loved to have gone to Sydney to be around them all. Her focus, however, was still on raising Dinah.

Then Ann's health deteriorated and Dinah, aged thirteen stepped up to help her out while James, three years Ann's senior was in good health and out working.

The news from Sydney early in 1822 was good. Henry had got himself a government job. Employed as the coxswain of the Row Guard on a salary of eighty pounds sterling a year.[359] This was an outstanding wage in the colony when you consider that a skilled tradesman in England was earning fifty five pounds per year.[360] His family were continuing to grow, and their Kent Street home was being improved all the time with the help of an assigned convict named Maurice Ahearn. In exchange for having the thirty-two-year-old Irishman assigned to him, Henry had to provide his food and shelter.[361]

The tide of good news had ended by spring, when Samuel's partner Bridget Cassidy was arrested as an accomplice to murder. The shock spread throughout the colony as the horrendous and gruesome details of the case came out. Ann must have felt a level of empathy for Samuel, who at fifty-seven was left with four young children to raise.[362][363] Bridget had just given birth to baby their son William when she found herself locked up. She had to wait in gaol for over a month until the trial began on the 12th of October.[364]

The victims, Samuel and Esther Bradley were an older couple who had just moved to their home at Birchgrove. It was five miles west of Sydney on the Balmain peninsula. On the 15th of August, their assigned convict, Thomas Barry, attacked Samuel Bradley, shooting him in the back then bashing him with the gun, killing him. Esther who had been in the city for the day returned in a boat that afternoon with her friend Margaret Hodges. Margaret stated at the trial that, Barry came to the landing-place and told them that Samuel had gone to Sydney after selling their pigs to some person on a ship. Esther felt something wasn't right and Margaret and the others on the boat stayed with her until sunset. Left alone after the boat departed, Barry then attacked and killed Esther, taking an axe to her.

[359] 'New South Wales, Australia, Colonial Secretary's Papers, 1788-1856 for Henry Howell 1822. Special Bundles, 1794-1825. Image 3000.' n.d. Ancestry. Accessed 14 May 2023. https://www. ancestry.com.au.
[360] The National Archives. n.d. 'The National Archives - Currency Converter.
[361] 'New South Wales, Australia, Returns of the Colony, 1822-1857 for Henry Howell., 1827. Image 44'. 1827. Ancestry. 1827. https://www. ancestry.com.au.
[362] 'Registers of Baptisms, Burials and Marriages, Series NRS 12937, Reel 5002, Baptism John Howell V1821330 8'. 1821. Museums of History New South Wales - State Archives Collection.
[363] ''New South Wales and Tasmania, Australia Convict Musters, 1806-1849 for Samuel Howell and Children 1822. General Muster. Image 311-312.' n.d. Ancestry. Accessed 13 February 2024. https://www.ancestry.com.au.
[364] 'New South Wales, Australia, Gaol Description and Entrance Books, 1818-1930 for Bridget Howel. Entrance Book, Sydney, 1819-1833. Image 111.' 1822. Ancestry. 3 September 1822. https://www. ancestry.com.au.

Figure 27: View from Birchgrove (1835) looking west up the Parramatta River. In the middle ground from left to right are the harbour islands of Snapper Island, Spectacle Island and Cockatoo Island-[365]

[365] Perry, Samuel Augustus. 1835. *View of Wrights Point Drummoyne, Hunters Hill and Harbour Islands, Parramatta River, New South Wales, ca. 1835 [Picture]*. National Library of Australia. https://nla.gov.au/nla.obj-134643203.

A few days after the murders Barry arranged to meet John Cochrane in Sydney. Cochrane was renting a room at Bridget's, and Barry, covered in scratches and blood met him there and hired Cochrane to move some goods. Barry, Cochrane and Bridget sat at Bridget's and drew up a list of the goods to be moved. The three of them then went out celebrating the deal at Michael Burns' pub in Pitt Street. Barry gave the publican a watch belonging to the Bradley's as security for their drinking debt.

While in town, Thomas Barry arranged with William Barry the watchman at the slaughterhouse to take delivery of some pigs. The two Irishmen conversed in their native tongue. Whether they were related or not is unknown.

Cochrane borrowed a boat nine days later and Thomas Barry directed him to Birchgrove where they loaded on the goods, including pigs. Barry wanted to unload the goods at the slaughterhouse wharf, but Cochrane said stock was already being unloaded there. He offered to store the goods in his room at Bridget's place, so they went to Mannix's Wharf at Cockle Bay instead.

Cochrane arranged for a cart to meet them there and they unloaded the goods from the boat with the help of William Barry. Cochrane and Thomas Barry proceeded to Bridget's where they unloaded the cart with the help of James Day. Bridget then directed Day to go and bring the five pigs from the boat.

Two weeks later the ransacked property at Birchgrove was noticed and "a bone was found in a putrefied state, supposed to have been the limb of some animal."[366] The chief constable was notified, and Samuel Bradley's body was discovered under a felled tree. It looked as if it had been burned and had been attacked by dogs. There was no sign of Esther's body.

It wasn't long before Cochrane heard the news of the gruesome crime and its location at Birchgrove. It must have been a sickening, gut churning shock. Realising that Thomas Barry was likely the killer and he had used him to get rid of the property. He immediately told a constable.

Barry was arrested and taken to the site where he pointed out the place that Esther was buried. The skull was smashed in and cut across the mouth. Barry blamed a man named Dennis Lamb for Samuel Bradley's murder and William Barry for Esther's.

These two were also arrested but were acquitted at the trial. William Barry was given a "most excellent character for attention to his duty"[367] by William Hill, his boss at the slaughterhouse. This was the same William Hill who was Henry Howell's father-in-law. Bridget was also acquitted as an accomplice. Thomas Barry found guilty was sentenced to death on Monday the 14th, with his body to "be delivered over to be disected (sic) and anatomized."[368]He made a full "confession on the scaffold."[369]

[366] *Sydney Gazette and New South Wales Advertiser*. 1822. 'Sydney.', 18 October 1822. 2. http://nla.gov.au/nla.news-article2181389.
[367] Sydney Gazette and New South Wales Advertiser. 'Sydney.', 18 October 1822. 4.
[368] Ibid.
[369] 'New South Wales, Australia, Colonial Secretary's Papers, 1788-1856 for Thomas Barry 14 Oct 1822. Main Series of Letters Received, 1788-1826. Image 13279.' n.d. Ancestry. Accessed 12 May 2023. https://www.ancestry.com.au.

Figure 28: Cockle Bay, now Darling Harbour[370]

[370] Taylor, James. 1819. *Cockle Bay Now Darling Harbour*. Mitchell Library, State Library of New South Wales.
https://collection.sl.nsw.gov.au/record/9PQ8wVrn/pXQ4allVKJJqX

On the 3rd of March 1823, at the age of fifty-four Ann died at Windsor and was buried two days later at St Matthew's churchyard under the name of Ann Howell. Her final resting place near the entrance of the church is the only physical evidence left of her existence and is a humble monument to her.

Figure 29: St Matthew's Church, Windsor with Ann's headstone in the foreground, 2023.

EPILOGUE

BISHOP THOMPSON

Bishop's fifty-acre land grand was measured out and documented on the 30th of June 1823. Located at Kurrajong about seventeen kilometres north-west of Windsor and nine kilometres north of Richmond. The land grant was a conditional grant, meaning Bishop was required to:

> clear and cultivate 15 acres of land within the term of 5 years, not to sell, aliene, assign, transfer or set over within the said term.
> Reserving to Govt the right of making Public roads through the same, also reserving for the use of the Crown the right of such Timber as may be deemed fit for Naval Purposes.[371]

By 1828 at the age of 52 he was listed as a labourer to Peter Hough of Richmond.[372] Hough had a neighbouring property.[373]

Bishop had probably been forced to give up his land grant after being unable to keep up with the conditions of the grant. The land was on a steep slope and was heavily timbered. Clearing fifteen acres at an advancing age would likely have been too physically demanding. No further record of Bishop has been found.

SAMUEL HOWELL

In 1826 Samuel was working as a publican when his clothes were stolen from a chest.[374] By 1828 he was sixty-three and viewed as an old man. He was listed in the census as working for son-in-law William Bruce as a blacksmith.[375] William was in Pitt Street and running a pub.[376] Samuel died and was buried on the 12th of May 1835 age seventy.[377]

JAMES HAGUE

James continued raising Dinah as a single parent for about eighteen months until circumstances changed and Dinah applied to marry Frederick Wilson.[378] It was

371 'New South Wales, Australia, Registers of Land Grants and Leases, 1792-1867 for Bishop Thompson 1823. Counties of Durham and Brisbane, 1823-1836 (Vol. 8). Image 63'. n.d. Ancestry. Accessed 7 March 2024. https://www.ancestry.com.au.
372 '1828 New South Wales, Australia Census (Australian Copy) for Bishop Thompson. (NRS 1272) 1828 Census: Alphabetical Return, Surnames L-T. Image 545'. n.d. Ancestry. Accessed 7 March 2024. https://www.ancestry.com.au.
373 'Historical Parish Maps. County: Cook, Parish: Currency. Sheet Referece:1, Edition: 2'. 2011. NSW Land Registry Services, Historical Lands Record Viewer. 2011. https://hlrv.nswlrs.com.au/.
374 Monitor. 1826. 'SYDNEY QUARTER SESSIONS.', 18 August 1826. 3. http://nla.gov.au/nla.news-article31757748.
375 '1828 New South Wales, Australia Census (TNA Copy) for Samuel Howell. New South Wales, Census E-H, 1828. Image 511'. n.d. Ancestry Accessed 7 March 2024. https://www.ancestry.com.au.
376 '1828 New South Wales, Australia Census (Australian Copy) for William Bruce. (NRS 1272) 1828 Census Alphabetical Return. Surnames A-C. Image 167'. n.d. Ancestry. Accessed 1 May 2023. https://www.ancestry.com.au.
377 'Registers of Baptisms, Burials and Marriages, Series NRS 12937, Reel 5004, Burial Samuel Howell V1835 1803 19'. 1835. Museums of History New South Wales - State Archives Collection.
378 'New South Wales, Australia, Colonial Secretary's Papers, 1788-1856 for Dinah Howell 1824, Copies of Letters Sent within The Colony, 1814-1827. Image 6442'. n.d. Ancestry. Accessed 7 March 2024. https://www.ancestry.com.au.

December 1824, and she may still have only been fourteen years old.[379] Thankfully the marriage never went ahead, and Dinah moved out to Hannah's place at Eastern Creek. Hannah had a six-month-old son named James Dean[380] and Dinah's help would have been invaluable. She was listed in the 1825 muster as being employed by Hannah's husband Thomas Dean.[381] She wasn't there for long because Thomas could not support her. He "was poor."[382] With no choice she moved back to Windsor, where her marriage to William Perry was soon arranged. Dinah explained what happened:

> With her father's approbation, [she] received the attentions of
> William Perry, a Government Servant of Mr Fitzgerald's of Windsor,
> and [her] father having obtained the Permission of the Government,
> in the usual way, thro' the medium of the Resident Chaplain [she]
> was married to the said William Perry.[383]

James was sixty and had resorted to using his carpentry skills to make and repair chairs.[384] He barely managed to make enough to live on.

A year after Dinah's marriage, Hannah's relationship with Tomas Dean fell apart. She left him and he said:

> she had, however, abandoned her home, and had taken with her a
> lovely babe, which had since been drowned, by carelessness of its
> nurse: that she had become the companion of another person; that
> she refused to return home.[385]

Thomas took her to court at Windsor in November 1826, where the magistrate "admonished and ordered [her] to return home and forsake her dissolute way."[386] She replied: "I beg to be excused, I cannot."[387]

For standing up for what she wanted and thereby defying the order, the magistrate sentenced her to be sent to the female factory for two months. She was five months pregnant at the time.

After her release she moved in with Richard Kippax and gave birth to William Henry Kippax on the 29th of March 1827.[388]

Richard was a thirty-six-year-old ex-convict, who was working as a wheelwright.[389] It was a trade with similar skills to those used by carpenters, and it provides us with an explanation as to why James was working with Richard in 1828.[390]

[379] No exact birthdate has been found for her but she was likely born in 1809-1810. See the narrative on her birth.
[380] Mutch. 'Reel 2127: James Dean Baptism and Burial, 1825 and 1826.'
[381] 'New South Wales and Tasmania, Australia Convict Musters, 1806-1849 for Dinah Egge, New South Wales. General Muster A-L 1825. Image 336'. n.d. Ancestry. Accessed 7 March 2024. https://www.ancestry.com.au.
[382] Sydney Gazette and New South Wales Advertiser. 1826. 'Police Reports.', 29 November 1826. 3. http://nla.gov.au/nla.news-article2187015.
[383] 'New South Wales, Australia, Convict Records, 1810-1891 for Dianna Perry 1826. Assignment and Employment of Convicts. Petitions from Wives of Convicts, Image 327.' n.d. Ancestry. Accessed 11 May 2023. https://www.ancestry.com.au.
[384] Ibid.
[385] Sydney Gazette and New South Wales Advertiser. 1826. 'Police Reports.', 29 November 1826. 3. http://nla.gov.au/nla.news-article2187015
[386] Ibid.
[387] Ibid.
[388] Mutch. 'Reel 2127: William Henry Egg or Kippey Baptism 1827'.
[389] '1828 New South Wales, Australia Census (Australian Copy) for Richd Keppars. (NRS 1272) 1828 Census: Alphabetical Return. Surnames C-L. Image 532'. n.d. Ancestry. Accessed 7 March 2024. https://www.ancestry.com.au.
[390] '1828 New South Wales, Australia Census (Australian Copy) for James Hayne. (NRS 1272) 1828 Census: Alphabetical Return. Surnames C-L. Image 375'. n.d. Ancestry. Accessed 7 March 2024. https://www.ancestry.com.au.

No further records mentioning James have been found until his burial registration nearly twenty years later. He died in the asylum as a pauper on the 7th of December 1849 at the grand old age of eighty-three.[391]

BRIDGET CASSIDY

By October 1825 Bridget had separated from Samuel and was starting to find herself in trouble again. She was violently assaulted by a man named Samuel Harris, but his sentence was lessened "on account of his general good character and on account of the character of the prosecutor, together with his having received some provocation."[392]

Sometime between 1826 and 1828 Bridget started a relationship with another Irish ex-convict named Andrew Gillis. They were raising the children in a "small wooden house at the corner of Bligh"[393] and Hunter Streets. Andrew had some cows and sold wood there. Bridget began trading in stolen goods from this new location and it wasn't long before she faced the law again.

On the 31st of January 1828 she walked west, a couple of blocks up Hunter Street to Francis Girard's bakery and coffee house. The Frenchman's business situated near the intersection with O'Connell Street aimed to bring a bit of Paris to Sydney, "where Pastry and Refreshments of any kind will be obtained."[394] Being a baker he had bran stored and hired men to produce flour. When Bridget got to the bakery, an employee named Mendoza asked what she wanted, and she said she needed to see the clerk to buy the bran. Another employee named Walter Hughes then filled her bag without measuring it. She paid him three shillings and left. Hughes pocketing the money went out and brought some rum and tobacco at Edward Franks', White Hart Inn just across the road from Bridget's house.

Franks' suspicions were raised, and he watched as Hughes crossed the road to Bridget's and the two of them left and headed back to the bakery. On arrival Hughes filled another bag for Bridget and she left without paying. Hughes, presumably wanting Mendoza to stay silent about the dealings, shared the rum. Bridget was seen by Franks returning with a bag full of bran and told the owner Girard what he had seen. Girard "procured the assistance of constables"[395]who searched her house and found the bran. Mendoza, Franks and Girard's testimonies the next day were enough to convict Hughes. Bridget was committed for trial at the Quarter Sessions which were to be held in April.[396]

Having her locked up was devastating for her children. Her daughter Mary Howell was sent to the Female Orphan School[397] and son Samuel remained with

[391] 'Registers of Baptisms, Burials and Marriages, Series NRS 12937, Reel 5011, Burial James Hague- V1849 971 34B'. 1849. Museums of History New South Wales - State Archives Collection.
[392] *Sydney Gazette and New South Wales Advertiser*. 1825. 'QUARTER SESSIONS.', 14 November 1825. 3. http://nla.gov.au/nla.news-article2184697.
[393]'Proceedings of the Supreme Court [Dowling], NRS5869'. 1837. Museums of History NSW - State Archives Collection.
[394] Dutton, Kenneth R. 2005. 'A COLONIAL ENTREPRENEUR: FRANCOIS GIRARD (17927-1859)'. *The French Australian Review* 39 (December). 12. https://www.isfar.org.au/category/explorations/no-39/.
[395] 'HOWELL Bridget in Quarter Sessions Cases 1824-1837 Sydney, Entry No 23 Item No [4/8449]'. 1828. Museums of History NSW - State Archives Collection.
[396] Ibid.
[397] 'New South Wales, Australia, Applications and Admissions to Orphan Schools, 1817-1833 for Mary Howell 1831. Female Admission Books. Image 13'. n.d. Ancestry. Accessed 20 March 2024. https://www.ancestry.com.au.

Andrew Gillis in Hunter Street.[398] The survival of sons John and William seems doubtful with no further records of them.

Two months into her wait, Francis Girard wrote a letter stating: "Oblige me to withdraw the prosecution which I have against Bridget Cacity (sic) before at the Quarter Session."[399]

Why the change of heart? He had been adamant in his testimony at Hughes' trial that bran found at her house was his bran and that it was stolen. Was someone pressuring him to recant? At her trial on the 15th of April, she was found guilty of receiving a quantity of stolen bran and knowing it to be stolen. There are comments on the trial paperwork which have no context and are curious clues that point to Girard being pressured. They are:

"I did not want to prosecute" and "after she asked you not to prosecute."[400]

She was sentenced to transportation for fourteen years and was taken to the female factory, where she spent twelve months before her sentence was mitigated due to an unspecified legal technicality. She was released on the 4th of June 1829 and went back to the house in Hunter Street, where she resumed her relationship with Andrew Gillis.

On the 27th of March 1832 Bridget wrote to the Commissioners managing the Female Orphan School appealing to get Mary released into her care. She said:

About three year and ten months back my Daughter Mary Howell
was sent to the female orphan school at the instance of the Rev.d Mr
Cowper on account of my being absent from Sydney for some time. I
therefore humbly entreat the Commissioners for an order to get my
Daughter out of the schools as I have sufficient means to educate
and support her.[401]

The request was denied. Four months later Andrew wrote to them saying:

I Humbly Request that Mary Howell a Girl now in the Female
Orphan School and Daughter of my Wife may be assigned to me.
I would also beg to state that I am in Business as a General Dealer,
resides in Hunter Street at the Corner of Bligh Street, Sydney. Is of
Honest, Industrious and Sober Habits.[402]

There is no indication if the request was successful, but Andrew's character proved to be anything but honest when he ended up in the hangman's noose.[403]

The details of his demise were reported in the papers and detailed in the Proceeding of the Supreme Court. As Christmas 1834 approached Andrew decided to hit the road and sell sly grog in the bush. The venture was so lucrative that Andrew sold his belongings in Hunter Street[404] and packed the family up, moving permanently to the Yass area. Accompanied by his employee John Kelly and an

[398] '1828 New South Wales, Australia Census (Australian Copy) for Samuel Howel. (NRS 1272) 1828 Census: Alphabetical Return. Surnames C-L. Image 435'. n.d. Ancestry. Accessed 20 March 2024. https://www.ancestry.com.au.
[399] 'HOWELL Bridget in Quarter Sessions Cases 1824-1837 Sydney, Entry No 23 Item No [4/8449]'. 1828. Museums of History NSW - State Archives Collection.
[400] Ibid.
[401] 'New South Wales, Australia, Applications and Admissions to Orphan Schools, 1817-1833. Application for Removal. Image 33'. 1832. Ancestry. 1832. https://www. ancestry.com.au.
[402] 'New South Wales, Australia, Applications and Admissions to Orphan Schools, 1817-1833. Application for Removal. Image 63.' 1832. Ancestry. 1832. https://www. ancestry.com.au.
[403] *The Australian.* 1837. 'Advertising', 21 February 1837. 3. http://nla.gov.au/nla.news-article36858314.
[404] *Sydney Gazette and New South Wales Advertiser.* 1835. 'Classified Advertising', 3 February 1835.3. http://nla.gov.au/nla.news-article2197226.

assigned convict they settled on a property next to William Roberts. He and his men would take to the road with his two carts loaded with casks of spirits and other goods. Staying away from the law, they sold to the isolated settlers. By April, Kelly was proving unreliable. Absenting himself without explanation. Andrew enlisted William Roberts' stockman, Jack Hoy to help him. When Kelly eventually returned, he asked for his severance pay. Andrew refused and Kelly threatened to report Andrew's illegal operations. After some arguments Andrew paid him and he left. Andrew and Hoy moved the carts on and were later approached by a customer who told them that the constables were coming to seize the rum and carts as evidence because "Kelly had given information."[405] They hid the alcohol and Andrew also hid. The constables seized his carts.

Andrew and Hoy then found out that Kelly had been deputised and armed to go and deliver summonses to Andrew's customers to appear in court. Andrew made up his mind to find Kelly and attempt to persuade him that if he continued then his carts would be confiscated, and he would be a "ruined man."[406] They did find Kelly and Andrew begged on his knees saying:

> *You have known me a long time; and having been an old servant of mine I hope you will not ruin me. I would sooner give you the £30 than give it to the Magistrate. I am afraid if you proceed in it, everything I have will be seized... and I shall be a ruined man.*[407]

Kelly agreed to take the payment and move on. Returning home together, the armed Kelly stopped for a drink at Jugiong Creek.[408] As he put the gun on the bank Andrew took advantage by picking up a rock and smashing Kelly's head. The feet and hands of the body were bound, and it was pushed into the waterhole. Hoy stated:

> *I did not tell of this for a year or better. I was in a queer part of the country & I was afraid to speak of it. I was afraid of him & other people.*[409]

Even though he said he was afraid he also said he could "have got away & given inf^n [information] but he persuaded me so hard that I did not."[410]

They returned the next day with a shovel to bury the body. With Kelly's disappearance the magistrate was unable to pursue the case of sly grog selling and Andrew's belongings were returned to him. Although Hoy claimed to be afraid of Andrew, he went into a partnership with him. Both men lived in fear. Andrew was plagued by nightmares. After twelve months Hoy went to the authorities and laid the accusation of murder against Andrew. He showed them where the body had been buried. Incredibly the skull was produced as evidence in the courtroom. Various people who knew Andrew when he lived in Sydney gave evidence about his character. Their testimonies throw light on his relationship with Bridget:

> *Mr Robert Campbell... 'He appeared always a quiet inoffensive man...He and his wife used to have a few squabbles. I don't know*

[405] *Sydney Monitor*. 1837. 'Law Intelligence', 15 February 1837. National Library of Australia. 2. http://nla.gov.au/nla.news-article32154892.
[406] Ibid.
[407] Ibid.
[408] 'Proceedings of the Supreme Court [Dowling], NRS5869'. 1837. Museums of History NSW - State Archives Collection.
[409] Ibid.
[410] Ibid

[if] he is a married man. He had a woman living with him as his wife'...

Mr Thos Shaughnessy... 'He appeared always a quiet man. I never heard of his being quarrelsome...quiet good tempered man'...

Mr Wm Roberts... 'I have known him quarrels with a woman he lived with'...

Mr Robert Clarke Snr... 'good tempered man. I used to be at his house often. He had a quarrelsome woman. Always quiet. They used to scuffle. Black eyes.'

Wm Dawes... 'He was a quiet industrious man. Always at work. Never disposed to quarrel'.[411]

Hoy's said in his testimony:

I did not charge Gillies with having a stolen mare or his wife: did not chge [charge] them with having stolen property in a chest...I did not accuse him & his wife all (sic) stolen property...There is a charge of cattle stealing agt [against] me. I know Gillies man & boy got it up.[412]

With no other family members found, the wife and boy must be Bridget Cassidy and Samuel Howell jnr.

Andrew was found guilty and hanged two days later. The newspapers reported that the body like that of all executed people was sent to the hospital where it was dissected and anatomized.[413] Horrifically, they report that one of his fingers was being passed around and shown at a pub later that night.[414]

Bridget had now been associated with two brutal murderers who had both ended up on the gallows with their bodies sent to the hospital to be used by doctors for training. Following Andrew's execution, she returned to Sydney. She continued selling goods and spent twenty-four hours in solitary confinement in May 1839 for drunkenness.[415] In 1857 at seventy-seven years of age she had her own shop in Glebe.[416] She died at the Benevolent Asylum three years later on the 15th of June 1860.[417]

ELIZABETH ALLEN

After arriving in Sydney on the *Mary Ann* she would have looked for her husband William. Not finding him she may have concluded he had been one of the many people who had died on the Second Fleet's horrendous journey out. Her enquiries may have given her some answers though. William would have been known by some of the convicts who had either been on board the prison hulk or the transport ship with him, people like Peter Larkham. The population were aware of

[411] Ibid
[412] Ibid
[413] *Sydney Gazette and New South Wales Advertiser*. 1837. 'MARKETS.', 18 February 1837. 2. http://nla.gov.au/nla.news-article2209473.
[414] *The Australian*. 1837. 'Advertising', 21 February 1837. http://nla.gov.au/nla.news-article36858314.
[415] 'New South Wales, Australia, Gaol Description and Entrance Books, 1818-1930 for Bridget Howell 1839, Entrance Book, Sydney, 1837-1841. Image 241'. n.d. Ancestry. Accessed 8 March 2024. https://www.ancestry.com.au.
[416] *Sydney Morning Herald*. 1857. 'CENTRAL POLICE COURT.', 8 December 1857.2. http://nla.gov.au/nla.news-article13003700.
[417] Murrin, Joy, trans. 2011. 'Transcript of New South Wales Death Certificate #858/1860 for Bridget McCarthy'.

the escape from Botany Bay because a search was initiated when they were discovered to be missing.[418] News of his survival and success in getting back to England however were not known. Governor Phillip only received a letter informing him of their arrival at England when the *Gorgon* arrived at Botany Bay[419] on the 21st of September 1791,[420] nearly three months after Elizabeth had arrived in the *Mary Ann*. Governor Phillip would not have made the news public for fear of encouraging other escape attempts.

Finding herself alone and with no chance of getting back to England, Elizabeth, like many married convicts, realised she would never see her spouse again and started a new relationship. John McIntosh was a Second Fleeter who had arrived on the *Neptune*. When their relationship began is unknown. The first reference of them living together was in the 1806 muster when she is listed as his wife.[421] They had no children.[422] It is probable that they had been together for many years as no prior relationships for either of them have been found.

They were living at the Hawkesbury and had been there for a number of years because John was on an 1802 list of people at the Hawkesbury with guns. He had one gun.[423] John had harvested his wheat and delivered it to the government store on the 22nd of April 1809 on the same day as Bishop.[424] The two men were listed close together on the delivery list so it would seem highly likely that Elizabeth and Ann would have still been in contact with each other.

They never had children and Elizabeth died five years before Ann in 1818[425], aged thirty-five. She was buried at St John's, Parramatta on the 11th of November.[426]

[418] Collins. An Account of the English Colony in New South Wales, 129.
[419] Bladen. Historical Records of New South Wales. Vol. 2. 475.
[420] Collins. An Account of the English Colony in New South Wales, 144.
[421] 'New South Wales and Tasmania, Australia Convict Musters, 1806-1849 for Elizabeth Allen. New South Wales, General Muster 1806. Image 35'. n.d. Ancestry. Accessed 8 March 2024. https://www.ancestry.com.au.
[422] Marsden, Samuel. 1806. 'Samuel Marsden Essays Concerning New South Wales.
[423] 'New South Wales, Australia, Colonial Secretary's Papers, 1788-1856 for John McIntosh 1802. Main Series of Letters Received, 1788-1826. Image 121'. n.d. Ancestry. Accessed 8 March 2024. https://www.ancestry.com.au.
[424] 'New South Wales, Australia, Colonial Secretary's Papers 1788-1856. Special Bundles 1794-1825. John McIntosh in Weekly Return at Hawkesbury 1809. Images 21133-21134'. n.d. Ancestry. Accessed 11 April 2023. https://www.ancestry.com.au.
[425] 'New South Wales, Australia, Settler and Convict Lists, 1787-1834, for Elizabeth Allen 1818. New South Wales, Female. Image 1-2'. n.d. Ancestry. Accessed 8 March 2024. https://www.ancestry.com.au.
[426] 'New South Wales, Australia, St. John's Parramatta, Burials, 1790-1986, for Elizabeth Allen 1818. Vol 01, Burials 1790-1825. Image 597'. n.d. Ancestry. Accessed 8 March 2024. https://www. ancestry.com.au.

Appendix 1
Family Tree

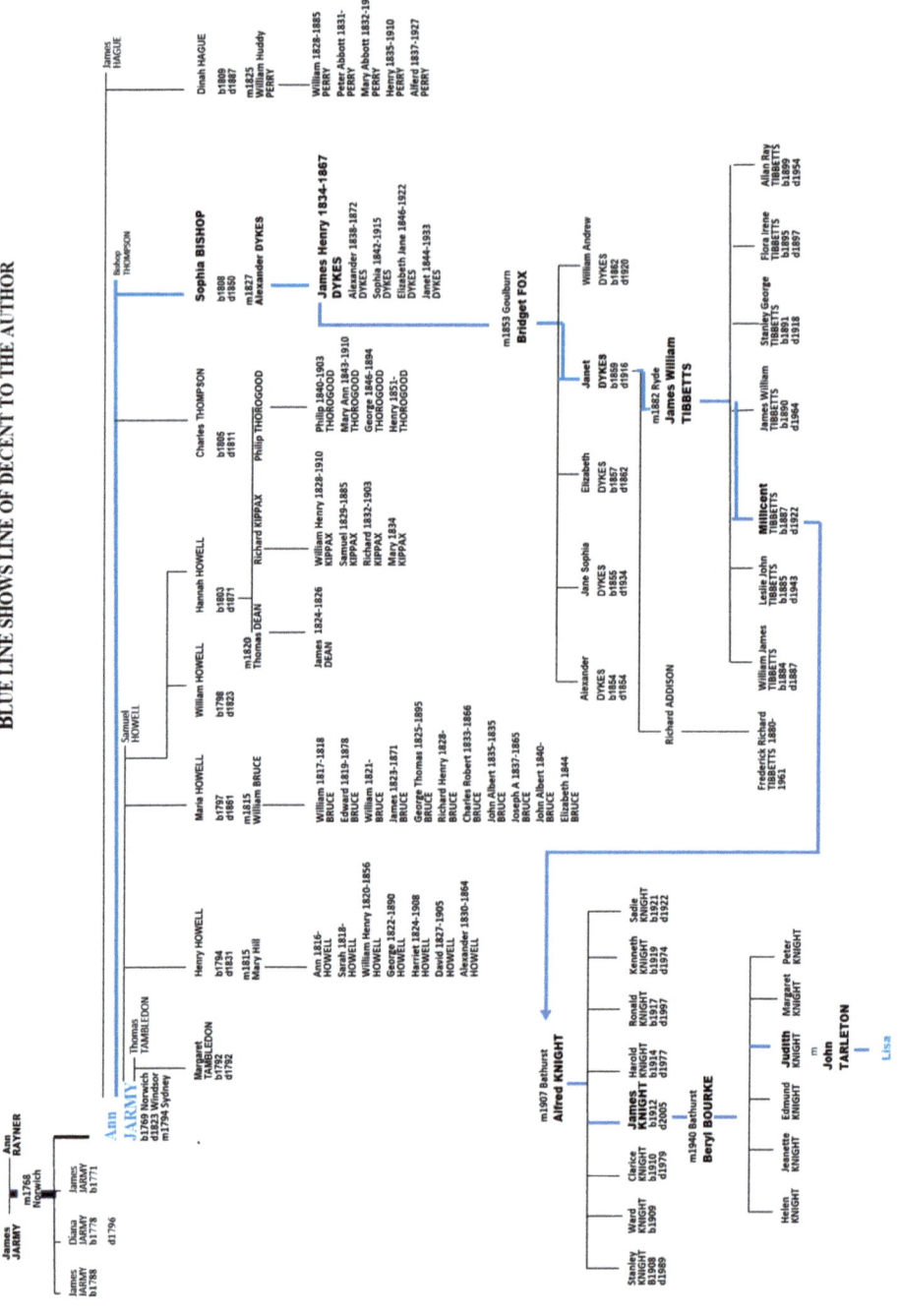

BIBLIOGRAPHY

'1788, and 1789, January to August'. 1789. *Home Office Papers and Records: Part One: HO 42, Box 14, 1782-1792.* https://link.gale.com/apps/doc/ALQWZC956572888/NCCO?u=nla&sid=bookmark-NCCO&xid=28255695.

'1828 New South Wales, Australia Census (Australian Copy) for Bishop Thompson. (NRS 1272) 1828 Census: Alphabetical Return, Surnames L-T. Image 545'. n.d. Ancestry. Accessed 7 March 2024. https://www.ancestry.com.au.

'1828 New South Wales, Australia Census (Australian Copy) for Henry Howell. (NRS 1272)1828 Census: Alphabetical Return. Surnames C-L. Image 436'. n.d. Ancestry. Accessed 24 April 2023. https://www.ancestry.com.au.

'1828 New South Wales, Australia Census (Australian Copy) for James Hayne. (NRS 1272) 1828 Census: Alphabetical Return. Surnames C-L. Image 375'. n.d. Ancestry. Accessed 7 March 2024. https://www.ancestry.com.au.

'1828 New South Wales, Australia Census (Australian Copy) for Maria Bruce. (NRS 1272) 1828 Census Alphabetical Return. Surnames A-C. Image 167'. n.d. Ancestry. Accessed 1 May 2023. https://www.ancestry.com.au.

'1828 New South Wales, Australia Census (Australian Copy) for Richd Keppars. (NRS 1272) 1828 Census: Alphabetical Return. Surnames C-L. Image 532'. n.d. Ancestry. Accessed 7 March 2024. https://www.ancestry.com.au.

'1828 New South Wales, Australia Census (Australian Copy) for Samuel Howel. (NRS 1272) 1828 Census: Alphabetical Return. Surnames C-L. Image 435'. n.d. Ancestry. Accessed 20 March 2024. https://www.ancestry.com.au.

'1828 New South Wales, Australia Census (Australian Copy) for Sophia Dykes. (NRS 1272) 1828 Alphabetical Return. Surnames C-L. Image 157.' n.d. Ancestry. Accessed 5 May 2023. https://www.ancestry.com.au.

'1828 New South Wales, Australia Census (Australian Copy) for William Bruce. (NRS 1272) 1828 Census Alphabetical Return. Surnames A-C. Image 167'. n.d. Ancestry. Accessed 1 May 2023. https://www.ancestry.com.au.

'1828 New South Wales, Australia Census (TNA Copy) for Samuel Howell. New South Wales, Census E-H, 1828. Image 511'. n.d. Ancestry. Accessed 7 March 2024. https://www.ancestry.com.au.

'16925; Original Letters from Various Writers, Relating to the "Association for Preserving Liberty and Property against Republicans and Levellers," Addressed to John Reeves, Chairman, and John Moore, Secretary, between 2 November, 1792, and 26 February,1793'. 1792. *Radicalism, Anti-Radicalism and Reform in England, 1769-1861: Original Papers and Minute Books: Original Papers and Minute Books from the Additional*

Manuscripts in the British Library, November.
https://link.gale.com/apps/doc/BUXIAX549423519/GDCS?sid=bookmar
k-GDCS&xid=242b0a44&pg=180.

Balmain, William. 1802. 'Series 23.03: Letter Received by Banks from William
Balmain.', 24 May 1802. Sir Joseph Banks Papers. State Library of New
South Wales. https://www.sl.nsw.gov.au/banks/section-06/series-23/23-
03-letter-received-by-banks-from-william.

Bath Chronicle and Weekly Gazette. 1791. 'London, Monday Feb. 14', 17
February 1791. The British Newspaper Archive.
https://www.britishnewspaperarchive.co.uk/viewer/bl/0000221/17910217/
007/0002.

Beresford, John. 1924. *The Diary Of A Country Parson*.
http://archive.org/details/in.ernet.dli.2015.227134.

Bladen, F.M., ed. 1892. *Historical Records of New South Wales (1783-1792)*. Vol.
1, Part 2. Sydney: Charles Potter, Government Printer.
https://nla.gov.au/nla.obj-343658027.

———, ed. 1892. *Historical Records of New South Wales (1793-1795)*. Vol. 2.
Sydney: Government Printer. 1892-1901. http://nla.gov.au/nla.obj-
359069774.

———, ed. 1895. *Historical Records of New South Wales (1796-1799)*. Vol. 3.
Sydney: Charles Potter, Government Printer. https://nla.gov.au/nla.obj-
359069148.

———, ed. 1901. *Historical Records of New South Wales. (1806, 1807, 1808)*.
Vol. 6. Sydney: Government Printer, 1892-1901.
https://nla.gov.au/nla.obj-375569940.

Cable v. Sinclair [1788] NSWKR 7; [1788] NSWSupC 7 - Macquarie Law School.
1788. NSW Supreme Court.

Caledonian Mercury. 1791. 'Plymouth March 24', 31 March 1791. The British
Newspaper Archive.
https://www.britishnewspaperarchive.co.uk/viewer/bl/0000045/17910331/
012/0003.

Catchpole, Margaret. 1809. 'Margaret Catchpole Papers, 1801-1870. Letter to Mrs
Cobbold from Richmond Hill.', 8 October 1809. Margaret Catchpole -
Papers, 1801-1870. State Library of New South Wales.
https://collection.sl.nsw.gov.au/record/nQR2o3L1.

Causer, Tim, ed. 2017. *Memorandoms by James Martin. An Astonishing Escape
from Early New South Wales*. London: UCL Press.
https://discovery.ucl.ac.uk/id/eprint/1558725/1/Memorandoms-by-James-
Martin.pdf.

Chase, William. 1783. *The Norwich Directory*. Norwich: W. Chase and Co.
https://www.gutenberg.org/files/62333/62333-h/62333-h.htm.

Clark, John Heavside, John Eyre, and D.D. Mann. 1810. *New South Wales, View of
Sydney from the East Side of the Cove*. National Library of Australia.
https://nla.gov.au/nla.obj-3084876277.

Collins, David. 1804. *An Account of the English Colony in New South Wales, from
Its First Settlement in January 1788 to August 1801*. 2d edition. Vol. 1.
London: Cadell & Davies.
https://www.biodiversitylibrary.org/item/172462.

'Colonial Secretary Index, 1788-1825 - Scarr, G to Schools (1820) for Phillip

Schaffer'. n.d. MHNSW. Accessed 18 March 2024.
  https://colsec.records.nsw.gov.au/s/F50c_sa-sf-06.htm#P2825_83231.
'Colonial Secretary's Papers 1788-1825. KABLE Henry, [9/2731], Pp.18, 48'.
  1794. Museums of History New South Wales - State Archives Collection.
  https://content.archives.nsw.gov.au/delivery/DeliveryManagerServlet?dps
  _pid=IE4136770.
'Colonial Secretary's Papers. HOWELL William [4/1824A], File No.376, p.405'.
  1820. Museums of History New South Wales - State Archives Collection.
  https://content.archives.nsw.gov.au/delivery/DeliveryManagerServlet?dps
  _pid=IE4149237.
'Convict Indents (Digitised) Index 1788-1801. HOWELL Samuel and WINBOW
  John, Ship Scarborough (2), Place of Trial: Winchester, County Hants'.
  1789. Museums of History New South Wales - State Archives Collection.
  https://content.archives.nsw.gov.au/delivery/DeliveryManagerServlet?dps
  _pid=IE378703.
Corr, Barry. 2015. 'Pondering the Abyss: A Study of the Language of Settlement
  on the Hawkesbury Nepean Rivers'. *Www.Nangarra.Com.Au*.
  http://pandora.nla.gov.au/pan/144576/20160201-
  0000/www.nangarra.com.au/documents.html.
Cotman, Miles Edmund. n.d. *View of Norwich - YCBA Collections Search*. Yale
  Center for British Art, Paul Mellon Collection. Accessed 24 February
  2024. https://collections.britishart.yale.edu/catalog/tms:8280.
'Court of Civil Jurisdiction. Andrew Thompson v Bishop Thompson, NRS 2659,
  Item 5/1103'. 1810. Museums of History NSW - State Archives
  Collection.
'Court of Civil Jurisdiction. Charles Beasley v Bishop Thompson, NRS 2659-2,
  Item 5/1110'. 1814. Museums of History NSW - State Archives
  Collection.
'Court of Civil Jurisdiction. H.C. Antill & T Moore Esqrs Exors v Bishop
  Thompson, NRS 2659-2, Item 5/1105'. 1811. Museums of History NSW -
  State Archives Collection.
'Court of Civil Jurisdiction. Lawrence May v Bishop Thompson, NRS 2659-2,
  Item 5/1108'. 1812. Museums of History NSW - State Archives
  Collection.
'Court of Civil Jurisdiction. Samuel Craft v Bishop Thompson, NRS 2659-2, Item
  5/1107'. 1812. Museums of History NSW - State Archives Collection.
Cunneen, Chris, and Mollie Gillen. 2005. 'John Black Caesar (c. 1763–1796)'. In
  Australian Dictionary of Biography. Canberra: National Centre of
  Biography, Australian National University.
  https://adb.anu.edu.au/biography/caesar-john-black-12829.
Dayes, Edward, and Thomas Watling. 1797. *[Western View of Sydney Cove,
  1797]*. https://nla.gov.au/nla.obj-134426258.
Derby Mercury. 1786. 'London, (Thursday) Sept. 14', 14 September 1786. The
  British Newspaper Archive.
  https://www.britishnewspaperarchive.co.uk/viewer/bl/0000189/17860914/
  003/0001.
———. 1792. 'London', 12 July 1792. The British Newspaper Archive.
  https://www.britishnewspaperarchive.co.uk/viewer/bl/0000052/17920712/
  017/0004.

'Devonshire Street Cemetery, Sydney for Mark Monro Death Date 18 Jun 1821.'
2021. Project Gutenberg Australia. 2021.
http://gutenberg.net.au/Devonshire-street/people/PersonPN14622.html.

Downes, Henry William. 1846. *Illustrated Log of the Whaling Barque TERROR*.
Object No 00038301. Australian National Maritime Museum.
https://collections.sea.museum/en/objects/details/11429/.

Dutton, Kenneth R. 2005. 'A COLONIAL ENTREPRENEUR: FRANCOIS
GIRARD (17927-1859)'. *The French Australian Review* 39 (December).
https://www.isfar.org.au/category/explorations/no-39/.

Earle, Augustus. 1827. *Cabbage Tree Forest, Illawarra, New South Wales*.
Watercolour. National Library of Australia. https://nla.gov.au/nla.obj-
134499059.

'ENGLAND AND WALES: Miscellaneous: Petition of George Robinson et al,
Booksellers, Asking...' 1796. The National Archives. 2 March 1796.
https://discovery.nationalarchives.gov.uk/details/r/C7666693.

Evans, George William. 1809. *Collection 03: View of Part of Hawkesbury River at
1st Fall and Connection with Grose River N.S. Wales*. Watercolour. State
Library of New South Wales.
https://collection.sl.nsw.gov.au/record/YRlZvN2n.

Eyre, J. 1804. *[View of Part of Sydney]*. National Library of Australia.
https://nla.gov.au/nla.obj-135178991.

Fletcher, B. H. 1967. 'James Ruse (1759–1837)'. In *Australian Dictionary of
Biography*. Vol. 2. Canberra: National Centre of Biography, Australian
National University. https://adb.anu.edu.au/biography/ruse-james-2616.

Flynn, Michael. 2016. 'Second Fleet'. The Dictionary of Sydney. 2016.
https://dictionaryofsydney.org/entry/second_fleet.

Ford, Lisa. 2010. *Settler Sovereignty : Jurisdiction and Indigenous People in
America and Australia, 1788-1836*. Cambridge, Mass. : Harvard
University Press. http://archive.org/details/settlersovereign00lisa.

Freycinet, Louis Claude Desaulses de. 1824. *Voyage Autour Du Monde, Entrepris
Par Ordre Du Roi. Exécuté Sur Les Corvettes de S.M. l'Uranie et La
Physicienne, Pendant Les Années 1817, 1818, 1819 et 1820. [Journey
around the World, Undertaken by Order of the King. Executed on the
Corvettes of H.M. Uranie and Physicienne, during the Years 1817, 1818,
1819 and 1820]*. Vol. [t.3] (1824) [Text]. Paris: Chez Pillet aîné.
https://doi.org/10.5962/bhl.title.152367.

'From Terra Australis to Australia. The Main Players - Macarthur, Bligh and
Johnston'. 2015. Text. State Library of NSW. 21 December 2015.
https://www.sl.nsw.gov.au/stories/terra-australis-australia/main-players-
macarthur-bligh-and-johnston.

'Further Memoirs of Rev. Richard Johnson (44pp), Papers of Archbishop John
Moore (as Filmed by the AJCP) [Microform] : [M677] 1793-1794./File
3'. 1794, 6 August 1794. Lambeth Palace Library.
https://nla.gov.au/nla.obj-859140416.

'Governor's Court Case Papers 1815-1824-Ann Howell and James Hague. Case
No 130, Series NRS 4563, Item No [4/7862] Index Number 76'. 1820.
NSW State Archives.

Griffiths, Tom. n.d. Artist's Impression of the Norwich City Walls on Their
Completion in 1343. Aviva Group Archive.

Harris, John. 1791. 'John Harris - Papers, 1791-1837', 20 March 1791. State Library of New South Wales. https://collection.sl.nsw.gov.au/record/Yj7dzlD9/mrLAKQKMb4O0x.

'Hawkesbury River, 1794, (File MPG 1/303. AJCP Reel No: 1546), (from Maps and Plans in the National Archives of the UK (as Filmed by the AJCP)'. 1794. National Library of Australia. https://nla.gov.au/nla.obj-1165150714.

Hereford Journal. 1791. 'Tuesday & Wednesday's Posts', 16 February 1791. The British Newspaper Archive. https://www.britishnewspaperarchive.co.uk/viewer/bl/0000397/17910216/007/0003.

'Historical Parish Maps. County: Cook, Parish: Currency. Sheet Referece:1, Edition: 2'. 2011. NSW Land Registry Services, Historical Lands Record Viewer. 2011. https://hlrv.nswlrs.com.au/.

'Holey Dollar'. undated. National Museum of Australia. undated. https://www.nma.gov.au/explore/collection/highlights/holey-dollar.

'HOWELL Bridget in Quarter Sessions Cases 1824-1837 Sydney, Entry No 23 Item No [4/8449]'. 1828. Museums of History NSW - State Archives Collection.

Hunter, John. 2005. *An Historical Journal of the Transactions at Port Jackson and Norfolk Island.* Project Gutenberg. https://www.gutenberg.org/ebooks/15662/pg15662-images.html.

Ipswich Journal. 1791. 'Friday's Post', 26 February 1791. The British Newspaper Archive. https://www.britishnewspaperarchive.co.uk/viewer/bl/0000191/17910226/005/0002.

Kable, Henry. 1809. 'Colonial Secretary's Papers, 1788-1825. Hawkesbury District. [SZ757], Pp57b-58b. Reel No. 6001', 5 August 1809. https://search.records.nsw.gov.au/permalink/f/1ebnd1l/INDEX2399108.

'Kable Henry: Bench of Magistrates Index 1788-1820 Item No: [SZ767] | Page No: 61 | COD: COD 77 | Reel No: 655'. 1799. Museums History New South Wales. NSW State Archives.

Karskens, Grace. 2020. *People of the River.* Crows Nest, NSW: Allen & Unwin.

King, Philip Gidley. 2015. 'Copy of a Chart Shewing the Inundation at the Hawkesbury March 22nd, 23rd, & 24th, 1806. Enclosure No. 2 / P.G.K.' [Sydney, N.S.W.][State Library of New South Wales]. State Library of New South Wales. https://collection.sl.nsw.gov.au/record/74VK7K6w3JoX.

Lake Macquarie Family History Group. 2003. *St Matthew's Church of England, Windsor, NSW.: Parish Registers, 1810-1856: 'A Complete Transcription'.* 1st ed. Vol. 1. Teralba, N.S.W.: Lake Macquarie Family History Group.

'Land Grants Guide, 1788-1856'. n.d. Museums of History NSW. Accessed 24 October 2023. https://mhnsw.au/guides/land-grants-guide-1788-1856/.

Lesueur, Charles Alexandre. 1807. *Timor, Vue de La Rade, de La Ville et Du Fort de Coupang (Kupang).* Engraving. National Library of Australia. https://nla.gov.au/nla.obj-150874947.

Lewis, Robert. 2009. 'Study Guide: The Floating Brothel. A Dramatised Documentary'. National Film and Sound Archive of Australia. 2009.

https://www.nfsa.gov.au/sites/default/files/05-2017/floating_brothel_tn.pdf.

Lloyd's Register Foundation, Heritage & Education Centre. 1792. *Lloyd's Register of Shipping 1792*. http://archive.org/details/HECROS1792.

Lycett, Joseph. 1817. *Aboriginal Australians Night Fishing by Fire Torches, New South Wales, ca. 1817*. Watercolour. National Library of Australia. https://nla.gov.au/nla.obj-138499378.

———. 1817. *Aborigine Climbing a Tree with Two Aborigines Sitting beside a Fire, Others Spearing Birds*. Watercolour. National Library of Australia. http://nla.gov.au/nla.obj-138498929.

———. 1817. *Aborigines Hunting Waterbirds in the Rushes*. Watercolour. National Library of Australia. http://nla.gov.au/nla.obj-138501323.

———. 1817. *Aborigines Using Fire to Hunt Kangaroos*. Watercolour. National Library of Australia. http://nla.gov.au/nla.obj-138501179.

Marsden, Samuel. 1796. 'S. Marsden (Parramatta) to [Unknown] (as Filmed by the AJCP) [Microform] : [M2686-M2696], 1795-1965./Fonds C 84/Series C 84/1', 16 September 1796. West Yorkshire Archive Service, Wakefield. http://nla.gov.au/nla.obj-1444999833.

———. 1806. 'Samuel Marsden Essays Concerning New South Wales, 1807-18--, with List of Females in the Colony, 1806?' State Library of NSW. https://collection.sl.nsw.gov.au/record/9O4olAAn.

Martin, James. 1794. 'Memorandom by James Martin Box 169 Folio 179-201'. Bentham Papers Database. http://transcribe-bentham.ucl.ac.uk/td/JB/169/180/001.

Monitor. 1826. 'SYDNEY QUARTER SESSIONS.', 18 August 1826. National Library of Australia. http://nla.gov.au/nla.news-article31757748.

Murrin, Joy, trans. 2011. 'Transcript of New South Wales Death Certificate #858/1860 for Bridget McCarthy'.

Mutch, T.D., and Genealogical Society of the Church of Jesus Christ of Latter-Day Saints. 1974. 'Mutch Card Indexes [Microform]. Reel 2125: 1787-1814 from Abbott to Tillet. Charles Thompson Burial 21 Sep 1811'. Central West Libraries.

———. 1974. 'Mutch Card Indexes [Microform]. Reel 2125: 1787-1814 from Abbott to Tillet. James Howell Baptism and Burial, 1809.' Central West Libraries.

———. 1974. 'Mutch Card Indexes [Microform]. Reel 2125: 1787-1814 from Abbott to Tillet. Margaret Tambleton Baptism and Burial'. Central West Libraries.

———. 1974. 'Mutch Card Indexes [Microform]. Reel 2125: 1787-1814 from Abbott to Tillet. Mary Howell Baptism'. Central West Libraries.

———. 1974. 'Mutch Card Indexes [Microform]. Reel 2125: 1787-1814 from Abbott to Tillet. Samuel Howell Baptism 1819'. Central West Libraries.

———. 1974. 'Mutch Card Indexes [Microform]. Reel 2125: 1787-1814 from Abbott to Tillet. Sarah Howell Baptism, 1818'. Central West Libraries.

———. 1974. 'Mutch Card Indexes [Microform]. Reel 2127: 1815-1957 from Curtis to Jurd. William Henry Egg or Kippey Baptism 1827'. Central West Libraries.

National Centre of Biography, Australian National University. n.d. 'Charles Williams (1762-1815)'. People Australia. Accessed 16 March 2024.

https://peopleaustralia.anu.edu.au/biography/williams-charles-29820/text36913.

'New South Wales and Tasmania, Australia Convict Musters, 1806-1849 for Dinah Egge, New South Wales. General Muster A-L 1825. Image 336'. n.d. Ancestry. Accessed 7 March 2024. https://www.ancestry.com.au.

'New South Wales and Tasmania, Australia Convict Musters, 1806-1849 for Elizabeth Allen. New South Wales, General Muster 1806. Image 35'. n.d. Ancestry. Accessed 8 March 2024. https://www.ancestry.com.au.

'New South Wales and Tasmania, Australia Convict Musters, 1806-1849 for Samuel Howell and Children 1822. General Muster. Image 311-312.' n.d. Ancestry. Accessed 13 February 2024. https://www.ancestry.com.au.

'New South Wales and Tasmania, Australia Convict Musters, 1806-1849 for Sophia Bishop 1822. New South Wales, General Muster, Image 46.' n.d. Ancestry Accessed 5 May 2023. https://www.ancestry.com.au.

'New South Wales and Tasmania, Australia Convict Musters, 1806-1849, New South Wales, General Muster. For Bishop Thompson. Image 123'. 1806. Ancestry. 1806. https://www.ancestry.com.au.

'New South Wales and Tasmania, Australia Convict Musters, 1806-1849, New South Wales, General Muster 1806. For James Hague. Image 72'. n.d. Ancestry. Accessed 5 May 2023. https://www.ancestry.com.au.

'New South Wales, Australia, Applications and Admissions to Orphan Schools, 1817-1833. Application for Removal. Image 33'. 1832. Ancestry. 1832. https://www.ancestry.com.au.

'New South Wales, Australia, Applications and Admissions to Orphan Schools, 1817-1833. Application for Removal. Image 63.' 1832. Ancestry. 1832. https://www.ancestry.com.au.

'New South Wales, Australia, Applications and Admissions to Orphan Schools, 1817-1833 for Mary Howell 1831. Female Admission Books. Image 13'. n.d. Ancestry. Accessed 20 March 2024. https://www.ancestry.com.au.

'New South Wales, Australia, Colonial Secretary's Papers, 1788-1856. For Ann Germay 12 Jun 1811- Special Bundles, 1794-1825. Image 1229'. n.d. Ancestry. Accessed 11 April 2023. https://www.ancestry.com.au.

'New South Wales, Australia, Colonial Secretary's Papers, 1788-1856 for Dinah Howell 1824, Copies of Letters Sent within The Colony, 1814-1827. Image 6442'. n.d. Ancestry. Accessed 7 March 2024. https://www.ancestry.com.au.

'New South Wales, Australia, Colonial Secretary's Papers, 1788-1856 for Henry Howell 1820. Memorials to the Governor, 1810-1826. Image 1690.' n.d. Ancestry. Accessed 15 May 2023. https://www.ancestry.com.au.

'New South Wales, Australia, Colonial Secretary's Papers, 1788-1856 for Henry Howell. Special Bundles, 1794-1825. Image 3000.' 1822. Ancestry. 21 February 1822. https://www.ancestry.com.au.

'New South Wales, Australia, Colonial Secretary's Papers, 1788-1856 for John McIntosh 1802. Main Series of Letters Received, 1788-1826. Image 121'. n.d. Ancestry. Accessed 8 March 2024. https://www.ancestry.com.au.

'New South Wales, Australia, Colonial Secretary's Papers, 1788-1856 for Samuel Howell 10 Sep 1818. Special Bundles, 1794-1825. Image 1270'. n.d. Ancestry. Accessed 4 May 2023. https://www.ancestry.com.au.

'New South Wales, Australia, Colonial Secretary's Papers, 1788-1856 for Thomas

Barry 14 Oct 1822. Main Series of Letters Received, 1788-1826. Image 13279.' n.d. Ancestry. Accessed 12 May 2023. https://www.ancestry.com.au.

'New South Wales, Australia, Colonial Secretary's Papers, 1788-1856 for William Bruce 1820. Memorials to the Governor, 1810-1826. Images 1172-1179.' n.d. Ancestry. Accessed 14 May 2023. https://www.ancestry.com.au.

'New South Wales, Australia, Colonial Secretary's Papers, 1788-1856 for William Hill 17 Sep 1817. Special Bundles, 1794-1825. Images 5448-5453.' n.d. Ancestry. Accessed 9 May 2023. https://www.ancestry.com.au.

'New South Wales, Australia, Colonial Secretary's Papers, 1788-1856 for William Howell 1820. Memorials to the Governor, 1810-1826. Image 1696.' n.d. Ancestry. Accessed 15 May 2023. https://www.ancestry.com.au.

'New South Wales, Australia, Colonial Secretary's Papers 1788-1856. Special Bundles 1794-1825. Bishop Thompson in Weekly Return at Hawkesbury 1809. Images 21133-21134'. n.d. Ancestry. Accessed 11 April 2023. https://www.ancestry.com.au.

'New South Wales, Australia, Colonial Secretary's Papers, 1788-1856. Special Bundles, 1794-1825. Image 18016-18017 for 1789'. n.d. Ancestry. Accessed 28 May 2022. https://www.ancestry.com.au.

'New South Wales, Australia, Colonial Secretary's Papers 1788-1856. Special Bundles 1794-1825. John McIntosh in Weekly Return at Hawkesbury 1809. Images 21133-21134'. n.d. Ancestry. Accessed 11 April 2023. https://www.ancestry.com.au.

'New South Wales, Australia, Convict Indents, 1788-1842 for Ann Jarmy. List of Convict Transports. 1790-1791 (Second Fleet and Part of Third Fleet). Image 30'. n.d. Ancestry. Accessed 22 April 2023. https://www.ancestry.com.au.

'New South Wales, Australia, Convict Indents, 1788-1842 for William Allen. List of Convict Transports, 1790-1791 (Second Fleet and Part of Third Fleet). Image 5.' n.d. Ancestry. Accessed 20 April 2023. https://www.ancestry.com.au.

'New South Wales, Australia, Convict Records, 1810-1891 for Dianna Perry 1826. Assignment and Employment of Convicts. Petitions from Wives of Convicts, Image 327.' n.d. Ancestry. Accessed 11 May 2023. https://www.ancestry.com.au.

'New South Wales, Australia, Convict Records, 1810-1891for James Hague. Musters, Muster of Prisoners in the Colony. For James Hague. Image 37'. n.d. Ancestry. Accessed 5 May 2023. https://www.ancestry.com.au.

'New South Wales, Australia, Gaol Description and Entrance Books, 1818-1930 for Bridget Howell 1839, Entrance Book, Sydney, 1837-1841. Image 241'. n.d. Ancestry. Accessed 8 March 2024. https://www.ancestry.com.au.

'New South Wales, Australia, Gaol Description and Entrance Books, 1818-1930 for Maria Bruce. Entrance and Description Book. Sydney. Image 463'. n.d. Ancestry. Accessed 1 May 2023. https://www.ancestry.com.au.

'New South Wales, Australia, Land Grants, 1788-1963 for Mary Howell 1831. Registrar General, Deeds Registration Branch, Registers of Memorials, 1826-1831. Image 228.' n.d. Ancestry. Accessed 10 May 2023. https://www.ancestry.com.au.

'New South Wales, Australia, Registers of Land Grants and Leases, 1792-1867 for
Bishop Thompson 1823. Counties of Durham and Brisbane, 1823-1836
(Vol. 8). Image 63'. n.d. Ancestry. Accessed 7 March 2024.
https://www.ancestry.com.au.

'New South Wales, Australia, Settler and Convict Lists, 1787-1834, for Elizabeth
Allen 1818. New South Wales, Female. Image 1-2'. n.d. Ancestry.
Accessed 8 March 2024. https://www.ancestry.com.au.

'New South Wales, Australia, Settler and Convict Lists, 1787-1834, New South
Wales. Male, for James Hague 1817. Image 219'. n.d. Ancestry. Accessed
13 June 2023. https://www.ancestry.com.au.

'New South Wales, Australia, St. John's Parramatta, Burials, 1790-1986, for
Elizabeth Allen 1818. Vol 01, Burials 1790-1825. Image 597'. n.d.
Ancestry. Accessed 8 March 2024. https://ancestry.com.au.

'New South Wales, Census and Population Books, 1811-1825 for Ann Germaine
1814. Population Muster. Image 38.' n.d. Ancestry. Accessed 5 May
2023. https://www.ancestry.com.au.

'New South Wales, Census and Population Books, 1811-1825 for James Hague
1814. Population Muster, 1814. Image 8'. n.d. Ancestry. Accessed 12
April 2023. https://www.ancestry.com.au.

'New South Wales, Census and Population Books, 1811-1825 for Maria Howell
1814. Population Muster. Image 127.' n.d. Ancestry. Accessed 9 May
2023. https://www.ancestry.com.au.

'New South Wales, Census and Population Books, 1811-1825 for Saml Howell
1814. Population Muster. Image 88.' n.d. Ancestry. Accessed 9 May
2023. https://www.ancestry.com.au.

'New South Wales, Census and Population Books, 1811-1825 for Will Howell.
Population Muster, 1819. Image 100'. 1819. Ancestry. 1819.
https://www.ancestry.com.au.

'New South Wales, Census and Population Books, 1811-1825 for Will Howell
1814. Population Muster. Image 96'. n.d. Ancestry. Accessed 9 May
2023. https://www.ancestry.com.au

'New South Wales Colonial Secretary; NRS-899 Memorials to the Governor,
1810-1826, Fiche 3032. Bishop Thompson to Governor Macquarie.
Pp791-792'. 1820, 1820. Museums of History New South Wales - State
Archives Collection.

'New South Wales Colonial Secretary's Papers, 1788-1825 for Bishop
THOMPSON. [4/1825B], File No.733, Pp.791-5.' 1820. Museums of
History New South Wales - State Archives Collection.

Norfolk Chronicle. 1779. 'Home News', 20 March 1779. The British Newspaper
Archive.
https://www.britishnewspaperarchive.co.uk/viewer/bl/0000246/17790320/
004/0002.

———. 1783. 'Home News', 8 February 1783. The British Newspaper Archive.
https://www.britishnewspaperarchive.co.uk/viewer/bl/0000246/17830208/
004/0002.

———. 1786. 'Friday's Post and Express.', 11 November 1786. The British
Newspaper Archive.
https://www.britishnewspaperarchive.co.uk/viewer/bl/0000246/17861111/
017/0002.

———. 1787. 'Friday's Post and Express.', 13 January 1787. The British Newspaper Archive. https://www.britishnewspaperarchive.co.uk/viewer/bl/0000246/17870113/004/0002.

———. 1787. 'London and Norwich Expedition', 12 May 1787. The British Newspaper Archive. https://www.britishnewspaperarchive.co.uk/viewer/BL/0000246/17870512/013/0003?browse=true.

———. 1787. 'Home News', 4 August 1787. British Library Newspapers. https://link.gale.com/apps/doc/GR3218759003/BNCN?sid=bookmark-BNCN&xid=8f3d4572.

———. 1789. 'Home News', 22 August 1789. British Library Newspapers. https://link-gale-com.rp.nla.gov.au/apps/doc/GR3218760764/BNCN?u=nla&sid=bookmark-BNCN&xid=c75d8484.

———. 1789. 'Friday's Post', 14 November 1789. British Library Newspapers. https://link-gale-com.rp.nla.gov.au/apps/doc/GR3218760942/BNCN?u=nla&sid=bookmark-BNCN&xid=ff3a48b1.

———. 1790. 'Friday's Post', 20 February 1790. British Library Newspapers. https://link-gale-com.rp.nla.gov.au/apps/doc/GR3218761182/BNCN?u=nla&sid=bookmark-BNCN&xid=f6b89f35.

———. 1790. 'Home News', 31 July 1790. British Library Newspapers. https://link-gale-com.rp.nla.gov.au/apps/doc/GR3218761640/BNCN?u=nla&sid=bookmark-BNCN&xid=6dcf408b.

———. 1791. 'News', 1 January 1791. British Library Newspapers. https://go-gale-com.rp.nla.gov.au/ps/navigateToIssue?volume=22&loadFormat=page&issueNumber=1040&userGroupName=nla&inPS=true&mCode=2FXF&prodId=BNCN&issueDate=117910101.

———. 1791. 'News', 5 February 1791. British Library Newspapers. https://link-gale-com.rp.nla.gov.au/apps/doc/GR3218762074/BNCN?u=nla&sid=bookmark-BNCN&xid=6af8fba4.

———. 1792. 'Bankrupts', 7 July 1792. British Library Newspapers. https://link-gale-com.rp.nla.gov.au/apps/doc/GR3218763291/BNCN?u=nla&sid=bookmark-BNCN&xid=3c892d27.

'Norfolk, England, Church of England Baptism, Marriages, and Burials, 1535-1812 for Ann Jarmy, Norfolk, Norwich, St Etheldreda. 1700-1781. Image 54.' 1778. Ancestry. 1778. https://www.ancestry.com.au.

'Norfolk, England, Church of England Baptism, Marriages, and Burials, 1535-1812 for Ann Jarmy 1769, Norfolk, Norwich, St Julian. 1723-1803. Image 64'. n.d. Ancestry. Accessed 19 April 2023. https://www.ancestry.com.au.

'Norfolk, England, Church of England Baptism, Marriages, and Burials, 1535-1812 for Bishop Thompson 1772. Norfolk, Norwich, St Giles. 1757-1812. Image 32'. n.d. Ancestry. Accessed 19 April 2023. https://www.ancestry.com.au.

'Norfolk, England, Church of England Baptism, Marriages, and Burials, 1535-1812 for James Jarmy, Norfolk, Norwich, St Etheldreda. 1700-1781. Image 54'. 1771. Ancestry. 1771. https://www.ancestry.com.au.

'Norfolk, England, Church of England Baptism, Marriages, and Burials, 1535-1812 for James Jarmy 1788, Norwich, St Julian, 1770-1853. Image 7.' n.d. Ancestry. Accessed 19 October 2023. https://www.ancestry.com.au.

'Norfolk, England, Church of England Baptism, Marriages, and Burials, 1535-1812, Ann Jarmy 1769. Norfolk, Norwich, St Etheldreda. 1700-1781. Image 54'. n.d. Ancestry. Accessed 19 April 2023. https://www.ancestry.com.au.

'Norfolk, England, Transcripts of Church of England Baptism, Marriage and Burial Registers, 1600-1935. Archdeacon Transcripts 1600-1812. Norwich City Parishes. Image 135, 1786 for William Allen and Elizabeth Curle'. n.d. Ancestry. Accessed 22 April 2023. https://www.ancestry.com.au.

'Norfolk, England, Transcripts of Church of England Baptism, Marriage and Burial Registers, 1600-1935 for Bishop Thompson 1771. Archdeacon Transcripts 1600-1812, Norwich City Parishes. Image 25'. n.d. Ancestry. Accessed 19 April 2023. https://www.ancestry.com.au.

Northampton Mercury. 1789. 'Wednesday & Thursday's Posts', 5 September 1789. British Library Newspapers. https://link-gale-com.rp.nla.gov.au/apps/doc/GR3218880687/BNCN?u=nla&sid=bookmark-BNCN&xid=067a5d12.

———. 1794. 'Wednesday and Thursday's Posts', 5 April 1794, Vol. 5, Issue 4 edition. British Library Newspapers. https://link-gale-com.rp.nla.gov.au/apps/doc/GR3218883688/BNCN?u=nla&sid=bookmark-BNCN&xid=3ed2e225.

'Old Register [Electronic Resource]:One to Nine: The Registers of Assignment and Other Legal Instruments. Book 4, P3a, Entry 269. 14 Aug 1809'. 2008. DVD-ROM. Kingswood, NSW: State Records Authority of New South Wales. State Library of Victoria.

'Old Register [Electronic Resource]:One to Nine: The Registers of Assignment and Other Legal Instruments. Book 4, P6, Entry 1250. 1 Oct 1804.' 2008. DVD-ROM. Kingswood, NSW: State Records Authority of New South Wales. State Library of Victoria.

Paine, Thomas. 1945. *The Complete Writings of Thomas Paine.* Edited by Philip S. Foner. New York: Citadel Press. http://archive.org/details/TheCompleteWritings.

Perry, Samuel Augustus. 1835. *View of Wrights Point Drummoyne, Hunters Hill and Harbour Islands, Parramatta River, New South Wales, ca. 1835 [Picture].* National Library of Australia. https://nla.gov.au/nla.obj-134643203.

'Proceedings of the Supreme Court [Dowling], NRS5869'. 1837. Museums of History NSW - State Archives Collection.

R. v. Powell [1799] NSWKR 7; [1799] NSWSupC 7. 1799. N.S.W. Court of Criminal Judicature.

'Registers of Baptisms, Burials and Marriages, Series NRS 12937, Reel 5002, Baptism Edward Bruce V1819 91 8'. 1819. Museums of History New South Wales - State Archives Collection.

'Registers of Baptisms, Burials and Marriages, Series NRS 12937, Reel 5002, Baptism John Howell V1821330 8'. 1821. Museums of History New South Wales - State Archives Collection.

'Registers of Baptisms, Burials and Marriages, Series NRS 12937, Reel 5002, Baptism Margaret Tambleton V1792163 4'. 1792. Museums of History New South Wales - State Archives Collection.

'Registers of Baptisms, Burials and Marriages, Series NRS 12937, Reel 5002, Burial Margaret Tambleton V1792465 4'. 1792. Museums of History New South Wales - State Archives Collection.

'Registers of Baptisms, Burials and Marriages, Series NRS 12937, Reel 5002, Burial William Bruce V1818 698 7'. 1815. Museums of History New South Wales - State Archives Collection.

'Registers of Baptisms, Burials and Marriages, Series NRS 12937, Reel 5002, Marriage Henry Howell V1815 151 7'. 1815. Museums of History New South Wales - State Archives Collection.

'Registers of Baptisms, Burials and Marriages, Series NRS 12937, Reel 5002, Marriage Maria Howell V1815186 7'. 1815. Museums of History New South Wales - State Archives Collection.

'Registers of Baptisms, Burials and Marriages, Series NRS 12937, Reel 5002, Marriage Samuel Holloway and Ann Jermie V1797244 4'. 1797. Museums of History New South Wales - State Archives Collection.

'Registers of Baptisms, Burials and Marriages, Series NRS 12937, Reel 5002, Marriage Thomas Dean and Hannah Howell V18202549 3A'. 1820. Museums of History New South Wales - State Archives Collection.

'Registers of Baptisms, Burials and Marriages, Series NRS 12937, Reel 5004, Burial Samuel Howell V1835 1803 19'. 1835. Museums of History New South Wales - State Archives Collection.

'Registers of Baptisms, Burials and Marriages, Series NRS 12937, Reel 5011, Burial James Hague- V1849 971 34B'. 1849. Museums of History New South Wales - State Archives Collection.

'Registers of Baptisms, Burials and Marriages, Series NRS 12937, Reel 5011, Burial James Hauge V1849 971 34B'. 1849. Museums of History New South Wales - State Archives Collection.

'Rev. R. Johnson (Sydney) to Gilpin. Fonds. Gilpin Papers/ Series MS Eng. Misc. c. 389/File Ff.252-54. (as Filmed by the AJCP)'. 1798, 5 November 1798. Bodleian Library. https://nla.gov.au/nla.obj-2060088120.

'Rev. Samuel Marsden (Sydney) to William Wilberforce (?) Papers of Archbishop John Moore (as Filmed by the AJCP)/File 4'. 1794, 4 May 1794. Lambeth Palace Library. http://nla.gov.au/nla.obj-1370817647.

Ryan, Lyndall. 2013. 'Untangling Aboriginal Resistance and the Settler Punitive Expedition: The Hawkesbury River Frontier in New South Wales, 1794–1810'. *Journal of Genocide Research* 15 (2): 219–32. https://doi.org/10.1080/14623528.2013.789206.

'Samuel Howell- Bench of Magistrates Index 1788-1820, Item No: [SZ766] P90, COD 76, Reel 655'. 1798. Museums of History NSW - State Archives Collection.

'Samuel Howell- Conditional Pardon [4/4430]; Reel 774 p 012'. 1800. Museums of History New South Wales - State Archives Collection.

'Scheyville National Park | Learn More'. 2023. NSW National Parks. 2023.

https://www.nationalparks.nsw.gov.au/visit-a-park/parks/scheyville-national-park/learn-more.

'Series 01: Australian Paintings by J.W. Lewin, G.P. Harris, G.W. Evans and Others, 1796-1809: Volume 3. f.7 "The Green Hills..."' 1809. Mitchell Library, State Library of New South Wales. https://collection.sl.nsw.gov.au/record/YoldQAA9/groKMN3JaexNk.

Shaw, A. G. L. n.d. 'Bligh, William (1754–1817)'. Australian Dictionary of Biography. Accessed 11 June 2022. https://adb.anu.edu.au/biography/bligh-william-1797.

Sillet, James. 1828. *Views of the Churches, Chapels, and Other Public Edifices in ... Norwich.* https://play.google.com/books/reader?id=0usHAAAAQAAJ&pg=GBS.PA1771&hl=en.

Smee, C J. 1790. 'Dr C J Smee's Early Colonial Australian 1788-1830 Database. Entry for Burial of Robert Murrell'. Fellowship of First Fleeters. 1790. http://www.fellowshipfirstfleeters.org.au/cjsmee_database/deadm_1.htm.

Stamford Mercury. 1790. 'STAMFORD, Aug. 6', 6 August 1790. British Library Newspapers. https://link-gale-com.rp.nla.gov.au/apps/doc/JA3230593991/BNCN?u=nla&sid=bookmark-BNCN&xid=90759bb0.

Steven, Margaret. n.d. 'Macarthur, John (1767–1834)'. Australian Dictionary of Biography. Accessed 11 June 2022. https://adb.anu.edu.au/biography/macarthur-john-2390.

'Story Map'. 2020. Dyarubbin: Mapping Aboriginal History, Culture and Stories of the Hawkesbury River, New South Wales. 2020. https://portal.spatial.nsw.gov.au/portal/apps/MapSeries/index.html?appid=82ae77e1d24140e48a1bc06f70f74269.

Sydney Gazette and New South Wales Advertiser. 1803. '1803', 5 March 1803. National Library of Australia. http://nla.gov.au/nla.news-page5653.

———. 1804. 'SYDNEY.', 15 July 1804. National Library of Australia. http://nla.gov.au/nla.news-article626311.

———. 1805. 'Classified Advertising', 24 March 1805. National Library of Australia. http://nla.gov.au/nla.news-article626697.

———. 1806. 'Bench of Magistrates.', 30 March 1806. National Library of Australia. http://nla.gov.au/nla.news-article627065.

———. 1806. 'HAWKESBURY, MARCH 27.', 30 March 1806. National Library of Australia. http://nla.gov.au/nla.news-article627063.

———. 1806. 'SYDNEY.', 30 March 1806. National Library of Australia. http://nla.gov.au/nla.news-article627066.

———. 1806. 'SYDNEY.', 13 April 1806. National Library of Australia. http://nla.gov.au/nla.news-article627080.

———. 1806. 'General Orders.', 24 August 1806. National Library of Australia. http://nla.gov.au/nla.news-article627259.

———. 1808. 'To the Printer of the Sydney Gazette.', 18 September 1808. National Library of Australia. http://nla.gov.au/nla.news-article627586.

———. 1808. 'Secretary's Office, December 17, 1808', 18 December 1808. National Library of Australia. http://nla.gov.au/nla.news-article627646.

———. 1809. 'SYDNEY.', 14 May 1809. National Library of Australia. http://nla.gov.au/nla.news-article627744.

——. 1809. 'FLOOD at HAWKESBURY.', 4 June 1809. National Library of Australia. http://nla.gov.au/nla.news-article627755.

——. 1809. 'Classified Advertising', 5 November 1809. National Library of Australia. http://nla.gov.au/nla.news-article627854.

——. 1809. 'Classified Advertising', 24 December 1809. National Library of Australia. http://nla.gov.au/nla.news-article627885.

——. 1811. 'Classified Advertising', 23 March 1811. National Library of Australia. http://nla.gov.au/nla.news-article628214.

——. 1814. 'Classified Advertising', 12 February 1814. National Library of Australia. http://nla.gov.au/nla.news-article628859.

——. 1816. 'GOVERNMENT PUBLIC NOTICE.', 23 November 1816. National Library of Australia. http://nla.gov.au/nla.news-article2176911.

——. 1819. 'GOVERNMENT AND GENERAL ORDERS.', 22 May 1819. National Library of Australia. http://nla.gov.au/nla.news-article2178714.

——. 1820. 'GOVERNMENT AND GENERAL ORDERS.', 20 May 1820. National Library of Australia. http://nla.gov.au/nla.news-article2179480.

——. 1822. 'Sydney.', 18 October 1822. National Library of Australia. http://nla.gov.au/nla.news-article2181389.

——. 1825. 'QUARTER SESSIONS.', 14 November 1825. National Library of Australia. http://nla.gov.au/nla.news-article2184697.

——. 1826. 'Police Reports.', 29 November 1826. National Library of Australia. http://nla.gov.au/nla.news-article2187015.

——. 1835. 'Classified Advertising', 3 February 1835. National Library of Australia. http://nla.gov.au/nla.news-article2197226.

——. 1837. 'MARKETS.', 18 February 1837. National Library of Australia. http://nla.gov.au/nla.news-article2209473.

Sydney Monitor. 1837. 'Law Intelligence', 15 February 1837. National Library of Australia. http://nla.gov.au/nla.news-article32154892.

Sydney Morning Herald. 1857. 'CENTRAL POLICE COURT.', 8 December 1857. National Library of Australia. http://nla.gov.au/nla.news-article13003700.

Taylor, James. 1819. Cockle Bay Now Darling Harbour. Mitchell Library, State Library of New South Wales. https://collection.sl.nsw.gov.au/record/9PQ8wVrn/pXQ4allVKJJqX.

Tench, Watkin and Royal Australian Historical Society. 1979. Sydney's First Four Years : Being a Reprint of A Narrative of the Expedition to Botany Bay and, A Complete Account of the Settlement at Port Jackson / by Watkin Tench ; with an Introduction and Annotations by L.F. Fitzhardinge. Sydney: Library of Australian History in association with the Royal Australian Historical Society.

The Australian. 1837. 'Advertising', 21 February 1837. National Library of Australia. http://nla.gov.au/nla.news-article36858314.

The History and Antiquities of the County of Norfolk. 1781. Norwich : Printed by J. Crouse for M. Booth. http://archive.org/details/b28745401_0010.

The National Archives. 1790. 'England & Wales, Crime, Prisons & Punishment Browse, 1770-1935, HO47, Judges' Reports On Criminals 1784-1830 - Correspondence, Piece13.' Findmypast. 31 July 1790. https://search.findmypast.co.uk/record/browse?id=TNA/CCC/HO47/013A/00308.

——. 1790. 'England & Wales, Crime, Prisons & Punishment Browse, 1770-

1935, HO13, Correspondence And Warrants, Piece7.' Findmypast. 4 August 1790. https://search.findmypast.co.uk/record/browse?id=TNA/CCC/HO13/007/00531.

———. n.d. 'How to Look for Records of...Criminal Transportation'. The National Archives. The National Archives. Accessed 19 April 2023. https://www.nationalarchives.gov.uk/help-with-your-research/research-guides/criminal-transportation/.

———. n.d. 'The National Archives - Currency Converter: 1270–2017'. Text. Currency Converter. The National Archives. Accessed 1 March 2024. https://www.nationalarchives.gov.uk/currency-converter/.

The Scots Magazine. 1793. 'Account Of Capt. Bligh's Expedition To The South Seas', 1 February 1793. https://www.britishnewspaperarchive.co.uk/viewer/bl/0000545/17930201/016/0035.

The World. 1792. 'Advertisements and Notices', 2 July 1792. Seventeenth and Eighteenth Century Burney Newspapers Collection. https://link-gale-com.rp.nla.gov.au/apps/doc/Z2001536624/BBCN?u=nla&sid=bookmark-BBCN&xid=d2dbc6e5.

Tompkin, Erin, and John Boyd. 2009. 'Scarborough Convict Transport'. Fellowship of First Fleeters. 2009. http://www.fellowshipfirstfleeters.org.au/ship_scarborough.htm.

Tozier, Josephine. 1904. *Among English Inns: The Story of a Pilgrimage to Characteristic Spots of Rural England*. Boston: L. C. Page & Company. https://link.gale.com/apps/doc/CYJJMG495400815/NCCO?sid=bookmark-NCCO&xid=b387a69d&pg=251.

'Trial of Charles Williams (T17840707-7)'. 1784. Old Bailey Proceeding Online. July 1784. https://www.oldbaileyonline.org/record/t17840707-7.

Wathen, Jonathan. 1790. 'Jonathan Wathen - Letter Received from William Hill, Sydney Cove, Port Jackson, 26 July 1790 (Copy Made in 1791)', 1791 1790. State Library of New South Wales. https://collection.sl.nsw.gov.au/record/9yMWVyx9.

Watling, Thomas. 1794. 'Letters From An Exile At Botany Bay, To His Aunt In Dumfries'. The University of Sydney Australian Digital Collections. University of Sydney Library. 1794. https://adc.library.usyd.edu.au/view?docId=ozlit/xml-main-texts/p00061.xml&chunk.id=d1324e262&toc.id=d1324e147&database=&collection=&brand=default.

———. 1794. *View of Sydney Cove*. Watercolour on paper. State Library of New South Wales. https://collection.sl.nsw.gov.au/record/nmQdrexn/8OZkB2xgBwWa4.

Watson, Frederick, ed. 1914. *Historical Records of Australia (1788-1796)*. Vol. 1. 1. Sydney: Library Committee of the Commonwealth Parliament. https://nla.gov.au/nla.obj-472896848.

———, ed. 1914. *Historical Records of Australia (1797-1800)*. Vol. 2. 1. Sydney: The Library Committee of the Commonwealth Parliament. https://nla.gov.au/nla.obj-739303274.

———, ed. 1914. *Historical Records of Australia (1801-1802)*. Vol. 3. 1. https://nla.gov.au/nla.obj-739469879.

————, ed. 1916. *Historical Records of Australia (January 1809 - June 1813)*. Vol. 7. 1. Sydney. https://nla.gov.au/nla.obj-469139834.

Whitcombe, Thomas. 1798. *Departure of the Whaler Britannia from Sydney Cove*. Painting: oil on canvas. National Library of Australia. https://nla.gov.au/nla.obj-134108884.

Whitehall Evening Post (1770). 1789. 'News', 1 September 1789. Seventeenth and Eighteenth Century Burney Newspapers Collection. https://link-gale-com.rp.nla.gov.au/apps/doc/Z2001627485/BBCN?u=nla&sid=bookmark-BBCN&xid=3fd14e6a.

Williford, James. 2010. 'Whaling The Old Way'. *Humanities the Magazine of The National Endowment for the Humanities*, April 2010. https://www.neh.gov/humanities/2010/marchapril/feature/whaling-the-old-way.

Wilson, Lowry. 1798. *Saunderson's Farm Looking down the River*. Engraving. National Library of Australia. https://nla.gov.au/nla.obj-135682235

INDEX

G

H

J

K

L

M

Ships

T

U

V

W

Milton Keynes UK
Ingram Content Group UK Ltd.
UKHW020754010824
446268UK00008B/37